KIT CARSON ON THE TRAIL

THE LIFE OF
KIT CARSON

THE GREAT WESTERN HUNTER AND GUIDE

By
CHARLES BURDETT

**Fredonia Books
Amsterdam, The Netherlands**

The Life of Kit Carson:
The Great Western Hunter and Guide

by
Charles Burdett

ISBN: 1-58963-694-5

Copyright © 2002 by Fredonia Books

Reprinted from the 1902 edition

Fredonia Books
Amsterdam, The Netherlands
http://www.fredoniabooks.com

All rights reserved, including the right to reproduce this book, or portions thereof, in any form.

In order to make original editions of historical works available to scholars at an economical price, this facsimile of the original edition of 1902 is reproduced from the best available copy and has been digitally enhanced to improve legibility, but the text remains unaltered to retain historical authenticity.

PREFACE.

In offering to the public a revised and complete history of the most remarkable of American frontiersmen, we perform a pleasing task. All the attainable circumstances connected with his life, adventures and death are fully set forth, and we offer this in confidence as a reliable authority for the reader.

No one should hesitate to familiarize himself with the exploits of the subject of this volume. They evince a magnanimity and an uprightness of character that is rarely found in one leading so daring and intensely wild a life, and cannot but contribute their share of luster to the interesting records of the Far West. We regret that his modesty, equally proverbial with his daring, prompted him to withhold many of the exciting incidents of his career from the public.

We have compiled a portion of this work from such official reports of his great skill, indomitable energy, and unfaltering courage as

PREFACE.

have been communicated by his friend and commander, Colonel Fremont, who has invariably awarded to him all the best attributes of manhood, when opportunity afforded. Added to these, our hero had been prevailed upon by a few of his friends to communicate some of the records of the most important passages in his extraordinary and eventful life, which are embodied in this volume.

His has indeed been a life of peculiarly exciting personal hazards, bold adventures, daring coolness, and moral and physical courage, such as has seldom transpired in the world, and we have been greatly impressed, in its preparation, with the necessity for a thorough work of this kind. All are aware that the young, and even matured, often seek for books of wild adventure, and if those of an unhurtful and truthful character are not found, they are apt to betake themselves to trashy and damaging literature. In this view, this work has a purpose which, we trust, will commend it to every family throughout the land.

INTRODUCTORY NOTE.

WHAT our modern age owes to men of the type of Christopher (Kit) Carson as an early explorer and guide in the Far West, when that region was but little known, and as a hunter and trapper when the recesses of the country were the abode almost entirely of wild beasts and equally wild and savage tribes, we are not always mindful of, though their history forms a heroic and fascinating part of the national annals. A marvellous change has now come over the scenes of the exploits of these early Western scouts and frontiersmen. Even Nature has experienced a transformation: the wild and wondrous life of those rough days has suffered a change; its savage charms have in the main disappeared, for the mountain lion is now rarely met with, while the grizzly bear, as Parkman tells us, " has shrunk from the face of man. His ferocious strength is now no match for the repeating rifle: he seeks the seclusion of his den, and has grown diffident and abated the truculence of his more prosperous days. In place, moreover, of Indian tepees, with their trophies of dangling scalplocks, we have now towns and cities, and the resorts of health and of pleasure-seekers."

INTRODUCTORY NOTE.

The story of Colonel Carson's intrepid life and labors as mountaineer, trapper, and guide, related by Mr. Burdett in the following pages, is full of thrilling incident. The narrative includes the story of his many Indian fights with Blackfeet, Comanches, Utes, Navajoes, and Cheyennes, and his important services in conducting General Frémont's various expeditions across the Rockies into California, and afterwards in acting as agent for the United States Government in New Mexico, Colorado, and Indian Territory, and in the Civil War in expeditions against the Confederates in Texas, and finally in making peace with the Navajo Indians. All this is told with graphic force and realistic description, as are the early accounts of Carson's exciting buffalo hunts, exploits in trapping and in the pursuit of the fur trade, and his keen zest and adventurous experiences in exterminating beaver. Not without interest, also, are the famous hunter's many trading ventures, including the purchase of some thousand sheep from the Navajo Indians and proceeding with them to Fort Laramie, thence, by way of the regular emigrant route to Salt Lake, across the mountains, on the farther side of which he disposes of them in California. Hardly less is the interest of the narrative in treating of Carson's career as an officer in the United States service during the Mexican war, as well as in the Civil War, in the latter of which he was rewarded with a brevet brigadier generalship. But perhaps most important of all was the aid he gave the National Government in his relations with

INTRODUCTORY NOTE.

the Indians of the Far West, whose tongue he spoke, and was well known to, and feared by, them as a mighty Indian fighter, though a man who could at the same time make a favorable peace with them, when the war-hatchet was thrown down and the calumet of peace was smoked by the smouldering campfire. Throughout his early career in the then wilderness stretches of Missouri, and in his adventurous roving life on the Plains, Carson's experience taught the great frontiersman many things of much benefit to him later on; but chiefly it developed in him mighty resources and phenomenal self-reliance, besides physical courage and hardihood, and gained for him the knack of picking up an intimate knowledge of Indian ways, and especially of the guile of native hostiles, that was subsequently of infinite service in his strenuous, diversified, and useful career. Added to these characteristics he had the virtues of honor, uprightness, and kindly feeling, as well as a frank manner and transparent truthfulness, which had their influence on all he came across, and, when death came to him, at Fort Lyon, Colorado, in May, 1868, won for his memory the benediction of those who best knew him.

G. MERCER ADAM.

LIFE OF KIT CARSON.

CHAPTER I.

As, for their intrepid boldness and stern truthfulness, the exploits and deeds of the old Danish sea-kings have, since the age of Canute, been justly heralded in song and story; so now, by the world-wide voice of the press, this, their descendant, as his name proves him, is brought before the world: and as the stern integrity of the exploits and deeds of the old Danes in the age of Canute were heralded by song and story; so too, in this brief and imperfect memoir, are those of one who by name and birthright claims descent from them. The subject of the present memoir, Christopher Carson, familiarly known under the appellation of Kit Carson, is one of the most extraordinary men of the present era. His fame has long been established throughout this country and Europe, as a most skilful and intrepid hunter, trap per, guide, and pilot of the prairies and mountains of the far West, and Indian fighter. But his celebrity in these characters is far surpassed by that of his individual personal traits of courage, coolness, fidelity, kindness, honor, and friendship. The theater of his exploits is extended throughout the whole western portion of the territory of the United States, from the Mississippi to the Pacific, and his associates have been some of the most distinguished men of the present age, to all of whom he has become an object of affectionate regard and marked respect. The narrative which follows will show his titles to this distinction, so far as his modesty (for the truly brave are always modest) has permitted the world to learn anything of his history.

It appears, from the various declarations of those most intimate with Christopher Carson, as well as from a biography published a number of years before his death, that he was a native of Madison County, Kentucky, and was born on the 24th of December, 1809. Colonel Fremont in his exhaustive and interesting Report of his Exploring Expedition to Oregon and North California, in 1843-44, says that Carson is a native of Boonslick County, Missouri; and from his long association with the hunter, he probably makes the statement on Carson's own authority. The error, if it is an error, may have arisen from the fact stated by Mr. Peters, that Carson's father moved from Kentucky to Missouri, when Christopher was only one year old. He settled in what is now Howard County, in the central part of Missouri.

At the time of Mr. Carson's emigration, Missouri was called Upper Louisiana, being a part of the territory ceded to the United States by France in 1803, and it became a separate State, under the name of Missouri, in 1821. When Mr. Carson removed his family from Kentucky, and settled in the new territory, it was a wild region, naturally fertile, thus favoring his views as a cultivator; abounding in wild game, and affording a splendid field of enterprise for the hunter, but infested on all sides with Indians, often hostile, and always treacherous.

As Mr. Carson united the pursuits of farmer and hunter, and lived in a sort of blockhouse or fort, as a precaution against the attacks of the neighboring Indians, his son became accustomed to the presence of danger, and the necessity of earnest action and industry from his earliest childhood.

At the age of fifteen, Kit Carson was apprenticed to Mr. Workman, a saddler. This trade requiring close confinement was, of course, utterly distasteful to a boy already accustomed to the use of the rifle, and the stirring pleasures of the hunter's life, and at the end of two years, his apprenticeship was terminated, for Kit, who, with his experience as the son of a noted hunter, himself perfectly familiar with the rifle, and, young as he was, acknowledged to be one of the best and surest shots, even in that State, where such merit predominated at that time over almost every other, could not bear in patience the silent, sedentary monotony of his life, voluntarily abandoned the further pursuit of the trade, and sought the more active employment of a trader's life.

His new pursuit was more congenial. He joined an armed band of traders in an expedition to Santa Fe, the capital of New Mexico. This, at that period, (1826,) was rather a perilous undertaking, on account of the Indian tribes who were ever ready to attack a trading caravan, when there was any prospect of overcoming it. No attack was made on the party, however, and no incident of importance occurred, if we except the accident to one of the teamsters who wounded himself by carelessly handling a loaded rifle, so as to render it necessary to amputate his arm. In this operation Carson assisted, the surgical instruments being a razor, an old saw, and an iron bolt heated red hot, in order to apply the actual cautery. Notwithstanding this rough surgery, the man recovered.*

In November (1826) the party arrived at Sante Fé, the capital, and the largest town in the then Mexican province of New Mexico. This place is situated on the Rio Chiuto, or Santa Fé river, an affluent of the Rio Grande, from which it is distant about 20 miles. It was then, as now, the great emporium of the overland trade, which, since 1822, has been carried on with the State of Missouri. The houses are chiefly built of *adobes*, or unburnt bricks, each dwelling forming a square, with a court in the center upon which the apartments open. This mode of building, originally Moorish, prevails in all the colonies settled by the Spaniards, as well as in Old Spain, and the oriental countries. It makes each house a sort of fortress, as General Taylor's troops learned to their cost at the siege of Monterey. The front entrance of each house is large enough to admit animals with their packs.

Santa Fé is well supplied with cool water from springs within its limits, and from fountains above the city near the neighboring mountain. The appearance of the place is inviting and imposing, as it stands on a plateau elevated more than 7,000 feet above the sea, and near a snow-capped mountain, which rises 5,000 feet above the level of the town; but the population is said to be exceedingly depraved. The present population is about 5,000; but at the time of Carson's first visit, it was comparatively a small town.

Soon after their arrival at Santa Fé, Carson left the trading band, which he had joined when he abandoned the saddlery business, or trade, as the reader may choose to term it, and of which we have previously spoken, and proceeded to Fernandez de Taos. In this place Carson passed the winter of 1826–7, at the house of a retired mountaineer. And it was while residing there, that he acquired that thorough familiarity with the Spanish language, which, in after years, proved of such essential service to him. In the spring he joined a party bound for Missouri, but meeting another band of Santa Fé traders, he joined them and returned to that place. Here his services being no longer required by the traders, he was again thrown out of employment. He now engaged himself as teamster to a party bound to El Paso, a settlement, or more properly a line of settlements, embracing a population of about 5,000, situated in the rich, narrow valley which extends 9 or 10 miles along the right bank of the Rio Grande, in the Mexican State of Chihuahua, 350 miles S. by W. of Santa Fé. Here the grape is extensively cultivated, and considerable quantities of light wine and brandy (called by the traders *Pass wine* and *Pass brandy*) are made. The houses are like those of Santa Fé, built of *adobes* with earthen floors. With abundance of natural advantages, the people are content to live without those appliances of civilized life, considered indispensable by the poorest American citizens. Glazed windows, chairs, tables, knives and forks, and similar every-day conveniences are unknown even to the rich among the people of El Paso. The place is the chief emporium of the trade between New Mexico and Chihuahua, and its name, "the passage," is derived from the passage of the river through a gorge or gap in the mountain just above the town.

On his arrival at this place, young Carson might justly be considered in view of his age (not yet 18), more than an ordinary traveler. He had arrived at a spot where everything was strange to him. New people, new customs, a new climate, a wine country, a population of mixed breed, half Indian, half Spaniard—everything wearing a foreign aspect; everything totally different from his home in Missouri.

He did not remain long in this place, but returned to Santa Fé, whence he again found his way to Taos, where he passed the winter in the service of Mr. Ewing Young, in the humble capacity of cook; this he soon forsook for the more pleasant and profitable position of Spanish interpreter to a trader named Tramell, with whom he, for the second time, made the long journey to El Paso and Chihuahua.

CHAPTER II.

CHIHUAHUA, where Carson had now arrived, is the capital of the Mexican province bearing the same name. It is situated on a small tributary of the Conchos River, in the midst of a plain. It is regularly laid out and well built the streets are broad and some of them paved. Like other cities built by the Spaniards, it has its great public square, or Plaza Major, on one side of which stands the cathedral, an imposing edifice of hewn stone, built at a cost of $300,000. It is surmounted with a dome and two towers, and has a handsome facade with statues of the twelve apostles, probably the first statues that Carson had ever seen. Other public buildings surround the square, and there is a fountain in the middle. The city contains a convent founded by the Jesuits, and an aqueduct 3½ miles long, supported by vast arches and communicating with the river Chihuahua. It has also its mint, and in the neighborhood are silver mines with furnaces for smelting the ore. It carries on an extensive trade with the United States by means of caravans to St. Louis in Missouri, and San Antonio in Texas. It was founded in 1691, and during the time when the silver mines were in successful operation, it contained 70,000 inhabitants. The population at present is 14,000.

As he had come with one of the trading caravans in the service of Colonel Tramell as Spanish interpreter, we might naturally expect that the engagement would be a permanent one. But such was not the case. The monotony of this life soon disgusted him, and after weary weeks passed in comparative idleness, he longed again for the freedom of the prairie and the forest, and gladly abandoning the rather dignified position of interpreter to Colonel Tramell, entered into the service of Mr. Robert M. Knight, in the more humble capacity of teamster in an expedition to the copper mines on the river Gila, whence he soon after found his way back to Taos.

It was during this visit to Taos that Carson was first enabled to gratify the desire which he had long entertained of becoming a regular hunter and trapper. A party of trappers in the service of Carson's old friend, Mr. Ewing Young had returned to Taos, having been beaten off from their hunting and trapping grounds by a hostile band of Indians. Mr. Young raised a party of forty men, for the double purpose of chastising the Indians, and resuming the business of trapping, and Carson joined them. The fact that he was accepted for this service was a marked token of esteem for his valor, as well as his skill in hunting, parties of this description always avoiding the enlistment of inexperienced recruits, as likely to embarrass their operations in the field.

The ostensible object of the expedition was to punish the Indians, but its ultimate purpose was to trap for beavers. The Mexicans by an express law had forbidden granting licenses to any American parties, and in this instance a circuitous route was chosen to conceal their real design.

They did not fall in with the Indians of whom they were in pursuit, until they had reached the head of one of the affluents of the Rio Gila, called Salt River. Once in presence of their enemies they made short work with them, killing fifteen of their warriors, and putting the whole band to rout. Such occurrences were by no means unfrequent, as we shall see in the course of this narrative. A small body of experienced hunters and trappers, confident in their superior skill and discipline, never hesitates to attack a greatly superior number of Indians, and it was a rare thing that success did not attend their daring. The Indian is not fond of a "fair stand-up fight." He prefers stratagem and ambush, and reverences as a great "brave" the warrior who is most successful in circumventing his enemies, and bringing off many scalps without the loss of a man; but when a considerable number of Indians are shot down in the first onset, the remainder are very apt to take to flight in every direction.

We have said that Carson joined the party of trappers under the command of Mr. Ewing Young, and it may not be out of place to describe briefly the mode of life which parties in that pursuit have to adopt, with a few remarks upon the habits and haunts of the animal, for whose sake men were then so willing to risk their lives, and to undergo such hardships.

The method of trapping for beaver formerly employed by the trappers in the western country is thus described by one who has had considerable experience in the art; and we quote it as illustrating the severe training to which Carson had voluntarily subjected himself:

"To be a successful trapper, required great caution as well as a perfect knowledge of the habits of the animal. The residence of the beaver was often discovered by seeing bits of green wood, and gnawed branches of the basswood, slippery elm, and sycamore, their favorite food, floating on the water, or lodged on the shores of the stream below, as well as by their tracks or foot-marks. These indications were technically called *beaver sign*. They were also sometimes discovered by their dams, thrown across creeks and small sluggish streams, forming a pond in which were erected their habitations.

"The hunter, as he proceeded to set his traps, generally approached by water, in his canoe. He selected a steep, abrupt spot in the bank of the creek, in which a hole was excavated with his paddle, as he sat in the canoe, sufficiently large to hold the trap, and so deep as to be about three inches below the surface of the water, when the jaws of the trap were expanded. About two feet above the trap, a stick, three or four inches in length, was stuck in the bank. In the upper end of this, the trapper excavated a small hole with his knife, into which he dropped a small quantity of the essence, or perfume, which was used to attract the beaver to the spot. This stick was attached by a string of horse hair to the trap, and with it was pulled into the water by the beaver. The reason for this was, that it might not remain after the trap was sprung, and attract other beavers to the spot, and thus prevent their going to where there was another trap ready for them.

"The scent, or essence, was made by mingling the fresh castor of the beaver, with an extract of the bark of the roots of the spice-bush, and kept in a bottle for use. The making of this essence was held a profound secret, and often sold for a considerable sum to the younger trappers, by the older proficients in the mystery of beaver hunting. Where they had no proper bait, they sometimes made use of the fresh roots of sassafras, or spice-bush; of both these the beaver was very fond.

"It is said by old trappers that they will smell the well-prepared essence the distance of a mile. Their sense of smell is very acute, or they would not so readily detect the vicinity of man by the smell of his trail. The aroma of the essence having attracted the animal into the vicinity of the trap, in his attempt to reach it, he has to climb up on to the bank where it is sticking. This effort leads him directly over the trap, and he is usually taken by one of the fore legs. The trap was connected by a chain of iron, six feet in length, to a stout line made of the bark of the leatherwood, twisted into a neat cord, of fifteen or twenty feet. These were usually prepared by the trappers at home or at their camps, for cords of hemp or flax were scarce in the days of beaver hunting. The end of the line was secured to a stake driven into the bed of the creek under water, and in his struggles to escape, the beaver was usually drowned before the arrival of the trapper. Sometimes, however, he freed himself by gnawing off his own leg, though this was rarely the case. If there was a prospect of rain, or it was raining at the time of setting the trap, a leaf, generally of sycamore, was placed over the essence stick, to protect it from the rain.

"The beaver being a very sagacious and cautious animal, it required great care in the trapper in his approach to its haunts to set his traps, that no scent of his feet or hands was left on the earth, or bushes that he touched. For this reason he generally approached in a canoe. If he had no canoe, it was necessary to enter the stream thirty or forty yards below, and walk in the water to the place, taking care to return in the same manner, lest the beaver should take alarm and not come near the bait, as his fear of the vicinity of man was greater than his sense of appetite for the essence. It also required caution in kindling a fire near their haunts, as the smell of smoke alarmed them. The firing of a gun, also, often marred the sport of the trapper, and thus it will be seen that to make a successful beaver hunter, required more qualities or natural gifts than fall to the share of most men."

CHAPTER III.

Carson's previous habits and pursuits had eminently qualified him to become an useful and even a distinguished member of Mr. Young's company of trappers. He had lived in the midst of danger from his childhood. He was familiar with the use of arms; and several years of travel and adventure had already given him more knowledge of the western wilds in the neighborhood of the region which was the scene of their present operations, than was possessed by many who had seen more years than himself. Added to this, he had become well acquainted with the peculiar character and habits of the western Indians, who were now prowling around their camp, and occasionally stealing their traps, game, and animals.

The party pursued their business successfully for some time on the Salt and San Francisco rivers, when a part of them returned to New Mexico, and the remainder, eighteen in number, under the lead of Mr. Young, started for the valley of Sacramento, California, and it was to this latter party Carson was attached. Their route led them through one of the dry deserts of the country, and not only did they suffer considerably from the want of water, but their provisions giving out, they were often happy when they could make a good dinner on horse-flesh. Near the Cañon of the Colorado they encountered a party of Mohave Indians, who furnished them with some provisions, which relieved them from the apprehension of immediate want.

The Mohave Indians are thus described by a recent visitor:

"These Indians are probably in as wild a state of nature as any tribe on American territory. They have not had sufficient intercourse with any civilized people to acquire a knowledge of their language, or their vices. It was said that no white party had ever before passed through their country without encountering hostilities; nevertheless they appear intelligent, and to have naturally amiable dispositions. The men are tall, erect, and well-proportioned; their features inclined to European regularity; their eyes large, shaded by long lashes, and surrounded by circles of blue pigment that add to their apparent size. The apron, or breech-cloth for men, and a short petticoat, made of strips of the inner bark of the cotton-wood, for women, are the only articles of dress deemed indispensable; but many of the females have long robes, or cloaks, of fur. The young girls wear beads; but when married, their chins are tattooed with vertical blue lines, and they wear a necklace with a single sea-shell in front, curiously wrought. These shells are very ancient, and esteemed of great value.

"From time to time they rode into the camp, mounted on spirited horses; their bodies and limbs painted and oiled, so as to present the appearance of highly-polished mahogany. The dandies paint their faces perfectly black. Warriors add a streak of red across their forehead, nose, and chin. Their ornaments consist of leathern bracelets, adorned with bright buttons, and worn on the left arm; a kind of tunic, made of buckskin fringe, hanging from the shoulders; beautiful eagles' feathers, called 'sormeh'—sometimes white, sometimes of a crimson tint—tied to a lock of hair, and floating from the top of the head; and, finally, strings of wampum, made of circular pieces of shell, with holes in the center, by which they are strung, often to the length of several yards, and worn in coils about the neck. These shell beads, which they call 'pook,' are their substitute for money, and the wealth of an individual is estimated by the 'pook' cash he possesses."

Soon after leaving the Mohave Indians, Mr. Young's party, proceeding westward, arrived at the Mission of San Gabriel. This is one of these extensive establishments formed by the Roman Catholic clergy in the early times of California, which form so striking a feature in the country. This Mission of San Gabriel, about the time of Carson's visit, was in a flourishing condition. By statistical accounts, in 1829, it had 70,000 head of cattle, 1,200 horses, 3,000 mares, 400 mules, 120 yoke of working cattle, and 254,000 sheep. From the vineyards of the mission were made 600 barrels of wine, the sale of which produced the income of upwards of $12,000. There were between twenty and thirty such missions in California at that time, of which San Gabriel was by no means the largest. They had all been founded since 1769, when the first, San Diego, was established. The labor in these establishments was performed by Indians converts, who received in return a bare support, and a **very** small modi cum of what was called religious instruction. Each mission had its Catholic priest, a few Spanish or Mexican soldiers, and hundreds, sometimes thousands of Indians.

The following interesting account of those of Upper California, we transcribe from a recent work of high authority.*

"The missions of Upper California were indebted for their beginning and chief success to the subscriptions which, as in the case of the missionary settlements of the lower province, were largely bestowed by the pious to promote so grand a work as turning a great country to the worship of the true God. Such subscriptions continued for a long period, both in Old and New Spain, and were regularly remitted to the City of Mexico, where they were formed into what was called '*The Pious Fund of California.*' This fund was managed by the convent of San Fernando and other trustees in Mexico, and the proceeds, together with the annual salaries allowed by the Crown to the missionaries, were transmitted to California. Meanwhile, the Spanish court scarcely interfered

Annals of San Francisco. By Frank Soulé, John H. Gihon, and James Nisbet. New York. D. Appleton & Co. 1855 with the temporal government of the country It was true that some of the ordinary civil offices and establishments were kept up; but this was only in name, and on too small a scale to be of any practical importance. A commandante-general was appointed by the Crown to command the garrisons of the presidios; but as these were originally established solely to protect the missions from the dreaded violence of hostile Indians, and to lend them, when necessary, the carnal arm of offense, he was not allowed to interfere in the temporal rule of the Fathers. He resided at Monterey, and his annual salary was four thousand dollars.

"In every sense of the word, then, these monks were practically the sovereign rulers of California—passing laws affecting not only property, but even life and death—declaring peace and war against their Indian neighbors —regulating, receiving, and spending the finances at discretion—and, in addition, drawing large annual subsidies not only from the pious among the faithful over all Christendom, but even from the Spanish monarchy itself, almost as a tribute to their being a superior state. This surely was the golden age of the missions —a contented, peaceful, believing people, abundant wealth for all their wants, despotic will, and no responsibility but to their own consciences and heaven! Their horn was filled to overflowing; but soon an invisible and merciless hand seized it, and slowly and lingeringly, as if in malicious sport, turned it over, and spilled the nectar of their life upon the wastes of mankind, from whence it can never again be collected. The golden age of another race has now dawned, and with it the real prosperity of the country.

"The missions were originally formed on the same general plan, and they were planted at such distances from each other as to allow abundant room for subsequent development. They were either established on the sea-coast, or a few miles inland. Twenty or thirty miles indeed seems all the distance the missionaries had proceeded into the interior; beyond which narrow belt the country was unexplored and unknown. Each mission had a considerable piece of the best land in the neighborhood set aside for its agricultural and pastoral purposes, which was commonly about fifteen miles square. But besides this selected territory, there was generally much more vacant land lying between the boundaries of the missions, and which, as the increase of their stocks required more space for grazing, was gradually occupied by the flocks and herds of the Fathers, nearest to whose mission lay the previously unoccupied district. Over these bounds the Fathers conducted all the operations of a gigantic farm. Their cattle generally numbered from ten thousand to twenty thousand and their sheep were nearly as numerous—though some missions had upwards of thrice these numbers—which fed over perhaps a hundred thousand acres of fertile land.

" Near the center of such farms were placed the mission buildings. These consisted of the church—which was either built of stone, if that material could be procured in the vicinity, or of *adobes*, which are bricks dried in the sun; and was as substantial, large, and richly decorated an erection as the means of the mission would permit, or the skill and strength of their servants could construct. In the interior, pic tures and hangings decorated the walls; while the altars were ornamented with marble pillars of various colors, and upon and near them stood various articles of massy gold and silver plate. A profusion of gilding and tawdry sparkling objects caught and pleased the eye of the simple congregations. Around, or beside the church, and often in the form of a square, were grouped the habitations of the Fathers and their household servants, and the various granaries and workshops of the people; while, at the distance of one or two hundred yards, stood the huts of the Indians. The former buildings were constructed of *adobes*, and covered with brick tiles, frail and miserable materials at the best. The huts of the Indians were occasionally made of the same materials, but more commonly were formed only of a few rough poles, stuck in the ground, with the points bending towards the center like a cone, and were covered with reeds and grass. An *adobe* wall of considerable height sometimes enclosed the whole village. The direction of the affairs of the settlement was in the hands of one of the Fathers, originally called a president but afterwards a *prefect;* and each prefect was independent in his own mission, and practically supreme in all its temporal, and nearly in all its spiritual matters, to any human authority.

"Thus the Fathers might be considered to have lived something in the style of the patharchs of the days of Job and Abraham. They indeed were generally ignorant and unlettered men, knowing little more than the mechanical, rites of their church, and what else their manuals of devotion and the treasuries of the lives of the saints taught them; but they seem to have been personally devout, self-denying, and beneficent in their own simple way. They thought they did God service, and perhaps much more the Indians themselves, in catching, taming, and converting them to Christianity. That was their vocation in the world, and they faithfully obeyed its calls of duty. Towards the converts and actually domesticated servants, they always showed such an affectionate kindness as the father pays to the youngest and most helpless of his family. The herds and flocks of the Fathers roamed undisturbed over numberless hills and valleys. Their servants or slaves were true born children of the house, who labored lightly and pleasantly, and had no sense of freedom nor desire for change. A rude but bounteous hospitality marked the master's reception of the solitary wayfarer, as he traveled from mission to mission, perhaps bearing some scanty news from the outer world, all the more welcome that the Fathers knew little of the subject, and could not be affected by the events and dangers of distant societies. All these things have now passed away. The churches have fallen into decay, deserted by the old worshipers, and poverty-stricken; the *adobe* houses of the Fathers are in ruins—and there is scarcely any trace left of the slightly erected huts of the Indians, who themselves have deserted their old hearths and altars, and are silently, though rapidly, disappearing from the land. But the memory of the patriarchal times, for they were only as yesterday, still remains fresh in the minds of the early white settlers."

Mr. Young's party did not remain long to enjoy the sumptuous fare at the Mission of San Gabriel; but pushed on to that of San Fernando, and thence to the river and fertile valley of Sacramento. In this neighborhood they trapped for beaver, and Carson displayed his activity and skill as a hunter of deer, elk, and antelope.

CHAPTER IV.

ONLY familiarity with one of like character, by actually seeing it, can give a just idea of the country through which they were traveling. Livingstone's descriptions of localities in Central Africa might be transferred to our pages *verbatim*, to give a word-painting of the desiccated deserts of what is now New Mexico and Arizona. Carson's curiosity, as well as care to preserve the knowledge for future use, led him to note in memory, every feature of the wild landscape, its mountain chains, its desert prairies, with only clumps of the poor artemisia for vegetation, its rivers, and the oases upon their banks, where there were bottom-lands — nor were beaver found elsewhere — with its river beds whose streams had found a passage beneath the surface of the earth, and each other general feature that would attract the eye of the natural, rather than the scientific observer.

In our day, the note-book of the pioneer furnishing the data, the traveler carries a guide book to direct his course from point to point, upon a well trodden road, to those places where grass and water will furnish refreshment for his animals, while he regales himself, not upon the spare-rib of a starved mule, killed because it could go no longer, but upon a variety of good things from the well stocked larder of the pouches of the saddle-bags his pack mule carries, or the provision box of his wagon. Or, instead of the meat-diet of the trapper, when he has been in luck in a fertile locality, the traveler—not trapper—of to-day, perhaps has shot a prairie chicken, and prepares his dinner by making a stew of it, which he consumes with hard bread he has purchased at a station not ten miles away.

Familiarity with the features of the country does not restore the experience of the pioneer of these wilds. The Indian, now, is advised by authority he seldom dares defy, to keep off the roads of the emigrants; and seldom does a party leave the road for any great distance; nor are these roads infrequent, but the country is intersected with them, and the guide-books protect against mistake in taking the wrong direction. The test of character, however, with the trappers, was their ability to endure hard ships when they had to be encountered; and to guard against them, when they could be avoided, by a wise foresight in taking advantage of every favor of fortune, and turning each freak or whim of the wily dame to best account.

Carson was delighted with California from the first, and realizing intense satisfaction in his position, yet a youth, on terms of easy familiarity with the other seventeen old trappers, especially selected for this expedition, circumstances conspired to call into play all the activities of his nature, and nothing intruded to prevent his resigning himself to the impulses of the time, and making the most of every occasion that offered.

He had the confidence of Captain Young and of all his men, who permitted him to do precisely as he chose, for they found him not only intending always to do what was best, but possessed of foresight to know always " just the things that ought to be done," almost without effort, as it seemed to them.

After leaving the Mission of San Fernando. Young's party trapped upon the San Joaquin, but they found that another party of trappers had been there before them, employed by the

Hudson Bay Company, in Oregon. There was, however, room for them both, and they trapped near each other for weeks. The friendly intercourse kept up between the two parties, was not only one of pleasant interchange of social kindness, but in one sense was essentially useful to Kit, who lost no opportunity of improving himself in the profession (for in those days trapping was a profession) which he had embraced, and he had the benefit of the experience by way of example, not only of his own companions, but of those who were connected with the greatest and most influential company then in existence on this continent. It is hardly necessary to say that he lost no opportunity of acquiring information, and it is quite probable that he would, if called on, allow that the experience acquired on this expedition was among the most valuable of any which he had previously gained.

When Mr. Young went to the Sacramento, he separated from the Hudson Bay party. The beautiful Sacramento, as its waters glided toward the chain of bays that take it to the ocean through the Bay of San Francisco out at the Golden Gate, had not the aspect of the eastern river's immediate tributaries of the

Missouri. Its waters then were clear as crystal, and the salmon floated beneath, glistening in the sunlight, as the canoe glided through them.

The very air of this valley is luxurious; and in speaking of it, we will include the valley of the San Joaquin, for both these streams run parallel with the coast, the Sacramento from the north, the San Joaquin from the south, and both unite at the head of the chain of bays which pour their waters into the Pacific.

The Sacramento drains nearly three hundred miles of latitude, and the San Joaquin an hundred and fifty miles of the country bounded by the Sierra Nevada (snow mountains) on the east, and the coast range on the west, the whole forming a great basin, with the mountains depressed on the north and south, but with no outlet except through the Golden Gate.

CHAPTER V

No climate could be more congenial to a full flow of animal spirits, than this region, where, upon the vegetation of the rich black soil—often twenty feet deep—game of the better class in great abundance found support. Deer in no part of the world was ever more plenty, and elk and antelope bounded through the old oak groves, as they may have done in Eden.

Carson had many opportunities of exploring the country, which he gladly embraced, and thus became familiar with many localities, the knowledge of which was in after years of such essential service to him and others.

There were many large tribes of Indians scattered through this country, in these and smaller valleys, beside those which the missions had attached to them. We know not that any record has been kept of the names of these tribes and their numbers; but since the white men intruded, they have melted away as did earlier those east of the Mississippi.

These Indians were all of the variety called Diggers, but in better condition than we see them, since the small remnants of large tribes have adopted the vices of the white men, and learned improvidence, by sometimes having plenty without much toil; so that they can say to-day, "No deer, no acorn; white man come! poor Indian hungry," as the happiest style of begging.

A brief description of the Tlamath or Digger Indians, and their mode of living, may not now be out of place, and having been visited by Carson in his earlier years, may not be uninteresting. We quote from the language of one who has paid a recent visit to the tribe:

"There were a dozen wigwams for the nearly hundred that composed the tribe, one of which was much larger than the rest, and in the center of the group, the temple, or 'medicine lodge.' As we entered, the bones of game consumed, and other offal lay about; and to our inquiry why they did not clear away and be more tidy, only a grunt was returned. The men had gone fishing, said the Indian women we addressed, so we saw but two or three; but in one wigwam which we entered there were fourteen with ourselves—the rest, besides the boy who went before to announce us, were women and children.

"We ascended a mound of earth, as it seemed, about six feet high, and through a circular hole, perhaps two feet and a half in diameter, descended a perpendicular ladder about ten feet. This opening, through which we entered, performed the double office of door and window to the space below, which was circular, about fourteen feet across, with arrangements for sleeping, like berths in a steamboat, one over another, on two sides, suspended by tying with bark a rough stick to upright posts, which served to hold the sticks that sustained the roof. The whole was substantially built, the covering being the earth which was taken from the spot beneath, heaped upon a layer of rushes, the floor of the wigwam being four feet below the surface of the ground. On the two sides of the wigwam not occupied by the berths, were barrels filled with fish—dried salmon, seeds, acorns, and roots.

"On hooks from the rush-lined ceiling hung bags and baskets, containing such luxuries as dried grasshoppers and berries. About the berths hung deer skins and some skins of other game, seemingly prepared for wear. There was no appearance of other dress, yet in the berths sat three women, braiding strips of deer-skin and attaching the braids to a string, in the form of long fringe. Each of the women wore an apron of this kind about the waist, and only the dress of nature beside. The children were dressed '*in puris naturalibus.*'

"After stopping ten minutes, we were glad to ascend to the open air, for a sickness came over us from which we did not recover for several hours. How human beings live in such an atmosphere we cannot tell, but this is the way they habitate.

"When the grasshoppers were abundant, for this insect is one of the luxuries of the Diggers, they scoured the valley, gathering them in immense quantities. This is done by first digging holes or pits in the ground at the spot chosen. Then the whole party of Indians, each with the leafy branch of a tree, form a circle about it and drive in the grasshoppers till they heap them upon each other in the pits: water is then poured in to drown them. Their booty gathered, they proceed to another place and perform the same operation. These insects are prepared for food by kindling a fire in one of these pits, and when it is heated, filling it with them and covering it with a heated stone, where they are left to bake. They are now ready for use at any time, and eaten with gusto, or they are powdered, and mixed with the acorn meal in a kind of bread, which is baked in the ashes."

To return to the camp of trappers, and witness one day's duties, may be gratifying to the reader. With early dawn the traps are visited, and the beaver secured. The traps are re-adjusted, and the game brought into camp—or left to be skinned where it is if the camp is far away. Meantime breakfast has been prepared by one of the party; others have looked after the animals, relieving the watch, which is still kept up lest a stampede occur while all are sleeping. Carson could not be cook for the party constantly, but takes his turn with the rest, and by the nice browning of his steak, and the delicacy of his acorn coffee, and the addition to their meal of roasted kamas root, he proves the value of the apprenticeship of his earlier years. He has a dish of berries, too, and surprises the party with this tempting dessert, as well as with the information that in his rambles the day before he had dined with an old Californian, with his wife and daughters, and had the promise from them of a cow, if he would call for it on the morrow.

Breakfast over, and the remains put by for lunch at noon, Carson mounts his pony, and riding a few miles down the bank, swims the river, and dashing out among the hills with a high, round mountain peak in view, still miles away, is lost among the oak groves for a score of miles, and at length emerges on Susan bay, and doffs his hat and makes his bow to the young Señorita who greets him at the door with a smile of welcome. The sun is low; dinner waits—hot bread, and butter, and cheese, and coffee, with sugar, are added to the venison and beef, and Irish and sweet potatoes. Amid the civilities and pleasant chat, the hour passes happily, and Carson proposes returning to his party.

The ladies will not allow him to depart. Will he not accept the hospitality of their mansion for a single night? They do not urge after one refusal, because his every feature indicates the decision of his character. He must go. His horse is brought—a young and beautiful animal—and the cow, this object of his second journey thither, given him in charge as he mounts, with a rope attached to her horns, by which to lead her. The full moon is rising, on which he had calculated, as he told his host-

esses, and with words of pleasant compliment.
with which the Spanish language so much more
than ours abounds, and a *Buenos noches, señor*,
from his entertainers, and *Buenos noches, señor-
itas*, in return, he slowly winds his silent way
on and on through the oak groves and the wild
oats covering the hill-sides, hearing only the
song of the owl and the whippoorwill, the music of the insects, and the whispering leaves,
but with ear ever open to detect the stealthy
tread of the monster of the wood and hills—the
grizzly bear. Off on the distant hill he sees
one, with a cub following her; but game is
plenty and deer is good enough food for her.
On, on he goes at slow pace, for he has a delicate charge, and already is she restive from
very weariness, though his pace is slow.

Half his journey is completed as the gray of
dawn and the twinkle of the star of morning
relieves the tedium and anxiety of his loneli-
ness. He has made the circuit of the bay.
The river is before him as he descends the hill
which he has ascended for observation. Morning broadens. The flowers glow with varie-
gated beauty as he tramples them, and in some
patches the odor of the crushed dewy beauties
fills the air to satiety.

A few miles more of travel and he crosses the river, and is again in the river-bottom where the party have taken the beaver. He stops at an Indian village, and dines from the liberal haunch and the acorn bread the chief presents, and with good feelings displayed on either side. takes in his arms a young papoose, the digger's picaninny, and salutes it with a kiss. Kit leaves there a trifling, but to them, valuable memorial of his visit, mounts his sorrel which is restive under the slow gait to which he has restrained him, takes the rope again which secures his treasure, the cow, and plods towards home at evening. The camp fire smokes in the distance, while the few horses that remain are staked about, and the sentinel paces up and down to keep off the drowsiness induced by fatigue and a hearty meat supper. The eastern and the western horizon are lighted with pale silver by the departing god of day, and the approaching goddess of the night, and the still river divides the plain, bounded only by the horizon, except he look behind him. Such is the scene as, approaching, the sentinel raises his gun and gives the challenge to halt. But the rest of the camp are not yet sleeping, and a dozen voices shout in the still evening a glad welcome to Carson, for whom they were not concerned, for they well knew there was not one of the party so well able to take care of himself as he.

CHAPTER VI.

PETERS, in his "Life of Carson," tells the story of two expeditions which Carson led against the Indians, while they trapped upon the Sacramento, which give proof of his courage, and thorough education in the art of Indian warfare, which had become a necessity to the *voyageur* on the plains, and in the mountains of the western wilds. With his quick discrimination of character, and familiarity with the habits of the race, he could not but know the diggers were less bold than the Apaches and Comanches, with whom he was before familiar.

The Indians at the Mission San Gabriel were restive under coerced labor, and forty of them made their escape to a tribe not far away.

The mission demanded the return of these fugitives, and being refused, gave battle to the neighboring tribe, but were defeated. The Padre sent to the trappers for assistance to compel the Indians not to harbor their people. Carson and eleven of his companions volunteered to aid the mission, and the attack upon the Indian village resulted in the destruction of a third of its inhabitants, and compelled them to submission. Captain Young found at this mission a trader to take his furs, and from them purchased a drove of horses. Directly after his return, a party of Indians contrived to drive away sixty horses from the trappers, while the sentinel slept at night. Carson with twelve men were sent in pursuit. It was not difficult to follow the fresh trail of so large a drove, yet he pursued them a hundred miles, and into the mountains, before coming up with them. The Indians supposed themselves too far away to be followed, and were feasting on the flesh of the stolen horses they had slaughtered. Carson's party arranged themselves silently and without being seen, and rushing upon the Indian camp, killed eight men, and scattered the remainder in every direction. The horses were recovered, except the six killed, and partly consumed, and with three Indian children left in camp, they returned to the joyful greetings of their friends.

Early in the autumn of 1829, Mr. Young and his party of trappers set out on their return home. On their route they visited Los Angeles, formerly called Pueblo de los Angeles, "the city of the angels," a name which it received on account of the exceedingly genial climate, and the beauty of the surrounding country. It is situated on a small river of the same name, 30 miles from its mouth, and on the road between the cities of San Jose and San Diego. It is about three hundred and fifty miles east of San Francisco, and a hundred miles to the south.

Although to very many thousands of readers, anything on the subject of the climate of California may seem superfluous, yet there are as many thousands who have no really distinct idea of the country or the climate, and we therefore quote from Rev. Dr. Bushnell, whose article on those topics in the "New Englander," in 1858, attracted justly such universal attention:

"The first and most difficult thing to apprehend respecting California is the climate, upon which, of course, depend the advantages of health and physical development, the growths and their conditions and kinds, and the *modus operandi*, or general cast, of the seasons. But this, again, is scarcely possible, without dismissing, first of all, the word *climate*, and substituting the plural, climates. For it cannot be said of California, as of New England, or the Middle

States, that it has a climate. On the contrary, it has a great multitude, curiously pitched together, at short distances, one from another, defying too, not seldom, our most accepted notions of the effects of latitude and altitude and the defenses of mountain ranges. The only way, therefore, is to dismiss generalities, cease to look for a climate, and find, if we can, by what process the combinations and varieties are made; for when we get hold of the manner and going on of causes, all the varieties are easily reducible.

"To make this matter intelligible, conceive that Middle California, the region of which we now speak, lying between the head waters of the two great rivers, and about four hundred and fifty or five hundred miles long from north to south, is divided lengthwise, parallel to the coast, into three strips, or ribbons of about equal width. First, the coastwise region, comprising two, three, and sometimes four parallel tiers of mountains from five hundred to four thousand, five thousand, or even ten thousand feet high. Next, advancing inward, we have a middle strip, from fifty to seventy miles wide, of almost dead plain, which is called the great valley; down the scarcely perceptible slopes of which, from north to south, and south to north run the two great rivers, the Sacramento and the San Joaquim, to join their waters at the middle of the basin and pass off to the sea. The third long strip, or ribbon, is the slope of the Sierra Nevada chain, which bounds the great valley on the east, and contains in its foothills, or rather in its lower half, all the gold mines. The upper half is, to a great extent, bare granite rock, and is crowned at the summit, with snow, about eight months of the year.

" Now the climate of these parallel strips will be different almost of course, and subordinate, local differences, quite as remarkable, will result from subordinate features in the local configurations, particularly of the seaward strip or portion. For all the varieties of climate, distinct as they become, are made by variations wrought in the rates of motion, the courses, the temperature, and the dryness of a single wind ; viz., the trade wind of the summer months, which blows directly inward all the time, only with much greater power during that part of the day when the rarefaction of the great central valley comes to its aid; that is, from about ten o'clock in the morning to the setting of the sun. Conceive such a wind, chilled by the cold waters that have come down from the Northern Pacific, perhaps from Behring's Straits, combing the tops and wheeling round through the valleys of the coastwise mountains, crossing the great valley at a much retarded rate, and growing hot and dry, fanning gently the foot-hills and sides of the Sierra, still more retarded by the piling necessary to break over into Utah, and the conditions of the California climate, or climates, will be understood with general accuracy Greater simplicity in the matter of climate is impossible, and greater variety is hardly to be imagined.

"For the whole dry season, viz., from May to November, this wind is in regular blast, day by day, only sometimes approaching a little more nearly to a tempest than at others. It never brings a drop of rain, however thick and rain like the clouds it sometimes drives before it. The cloud element, indeed, is always in it. Sometimes it is floated above, in the manner commonly designated by the term *cloud*. Sometimes, as in the early morning, when the wind is most quiet, it may be seen as a kind of fog bank resting on the sea-wall mountains or rolling down landward through the interstices of their summits. When the wind begins to hurry and take on less composedly, the fog becomes blown fog, a kind of lead dust driven through the air, reducing it from a transparent to a semi-transparent or merely translucent state, so that if any one looks up the bay, from a point twenty or thirty miles south of San Francisco, in the afternoon, he will commonly see, directly abreast of the Golden Gate where this wind drives in with its greatest power, a pencil of the lead dust shooting upwards at an angle of thirty or forty degrees (which is the aim of the wind preparing to leap the second chain of mountains, the other side of the bay), and finally tapering off and vanishing, at a mid-air point eight or ten miles inland, where the increased heat of the atmosphere has taken up the moisture, and restored its complete transparency. This wind is so cold, that one who will sit upon the deck of the afternoon steamer passing up the bay, will even require his heaviest winter clothing. And so rough are the waters of the bay, landlocked and narrow as it is, that sea-sickness is a kind of regular experience, with such as are candidates for that kind of felicity.

" We return now to the middle strip of the great valley where the engine, or rather boiler power, that operates the coast wind in a great part of its velocity, is located. Here the heat, reverberated as in a forge, or oven (whence *Cali—fornia*) becomes, even in the early spring so much raised that the ground is no longer able, by any remaining cold there is in it, to condense the clouds, and rain ceases. A little further on in the season, there is not cooling influence enough left to allow even the phenomena of cloud, and for weeks together, not a cloud will be seen, unless, by chance, the skirt of one may just appear now and then, hanging over the summit of the western mountains. The sun rises, fixing his hot stare on the world, and stares through the day. Then he returns as in an orrery, and stares through another, in exactly the same way. The thermometer will go up, not seldom, to 100° or even 110°, and judging by what we know of effects here in New England, we should suppose that life would scarcely be supportable. And yet there is much less suffering from heat in this valley than with us, for the reason probably that the nights are uniformly cool. The thermometer goes down regularly with the sun, and one or two blankets are wanted for the comfort of the night. This cooling of the night is probably determined by the fact that the cool sea wind sweeping through the upper air of the valley, from the coast mountains on one side, over the mountains and mountain passes of the Sierra on the other, is not able to get down to the ground of the valley during the day, because of the powerfully steaming column of heat that rises from it; but as soon as the sun goes down, it drops immediately to the level of the plain, bathing it for the night with a kind of perpendicular sea breeze, that has lost for the time a great part of its lateral motion. The consequence is that no one is greatly debilitated by the heat. On the contrary, it is the general testimony, that a man can do as much of mental or bodily labor in this climate, as in any other. And it is a good confirmation of this opinion, that horses will here maintain a wonderful energy, traveling greater distances, complaining far less of heat, and sustaining their spirit a great deal better than with us. It is also to be noted that there is no special tendency to fevers in this hot region, except in what is called the *tule* bottom, a kind of giant bulrush region, along the most depressed and marshiest portions of the rivers.

"Passing now to the eastern strip or portion,

the slope of the Nevada, the heat, except in those deep cañons where the reverberation makes it sometimes even insupportable, is qualified in degree, according to the altitude. A gentle west wind, warmer in the lower parts or foothills by the heat of the valley, fans it all day. At points which are higher, the wind is cooler; but here also, on the slope of the Nevada, the nights are always cool in summer, so cool, that the late and early frosts leave too short a space for the ordinary summer crop to mature, even where the altitude is not more than 3,000 or 4,000 feet. Meantime, at the top of the Sierra, where the west wind, piling up from below, breaks over into Utah, travelers undertake to say that in some of the passes it blows with such stress as even to polish the rocks, by the gravel and sand which it drives before it. The day is cloudless on the slope of the Sierra, as in the valley; but on the top there is now and then, or once in a year or two, a moderate thunder shower. With this exception, as referring to a part uninhabitable, thunder is scarcely ever heard in California. The principal thunders of California are underground.

" We return now to the coast-wise mountain region, where the multiplicity and confusion of climates is most remarkable. Their variety we shall find depends on the courses of the wind currents, turned hither and thither by the mountains; partly also on the side any given place occupies of its valley or mountain; and partly on the proximity of the sea. Sprinkled in among these mountains, and more or less enclosed by them, are valleys, large and small, of the highest beauty. But a valley in California means something more than a scoop or depression. It means a rich land-lake, leveled between the mountains, with a sharply defined, picturesque shore, where it meets the sides and runs into the indentations of the mountains. What is called the Bay of San Francisco, is a large salt water lake in the middle of a much larger land-lake, sometimes called the San Jose valley. It extends south of the city forty miles, and northward among islands and mountains about twenty-five more, if we include what is called San Pueblo Bay. Three beautiful valleys of agricultural country, the Petaluma, Sonora, and Napa valleys, open into this larger valley of the bay, on the north end of it between four mountain barriers, having each a short navigable creek or inlet. Still farther north is the Russian River valley, opening towards the sea, and the Clear Lake valley and region, which is the Switzerland of California. East of the San Jose valley, too, at the foot of Diabola, and up among the mountains, are the large Amador and San Ramon valleys, also the little gem of the Suñole. Now these valleys which, if we except the great valley of two rivers, comprise the plow-land of Middle California, have each a climate of its own, and productions that correspond. We have only to observe further, that the east side of any valley will commonly be much warmer than the west for the very paradoxical reason that the cold coast-wind always blows much harder on the other side or steep slope even, of a mountain, opposite or away from the wind, than it does on the side towards it, reversing all our notions of the sheltering effects of mountain ridges.

CHAPTER VII

DURING this brief tarry at Los Angeles, Carson had not been idle, but entirely without thought that his confidence could be deemed presumption, arranging his dress with as much care as its character permitted, early in the morning he mounted his horse—always in excellent trim—and rode to the residence of the man he had been informed owned the best *ranche* in the vicinity, and dismounting at the wicket gate, entered the yard, which was fenced with a finely arranged growth of club cactus; and passing up the gravel walk several rods, between an avenue of fig trees, with an occasional patch of green shrubs, and a few flowers, he stood at the door of the spacious old Spanish mansion, which was built of *adobe* one story in height and nearly a hundred feet in length, its roof covered with asphaltum mingled with sand —like all the houses in Los Angeles, a spring of this material existing a little way from the town. After waiting a few moments for an answer to his summons, made with the huge brass knocker, an Indian servant made his appearance, and ushered him to an elegantly furnished room, with several guitars lying about as if recently in use. The lordly owner of the ranche soon appeared in morning gown and slippers, the picture of a well-to-do old-time gentleman, with an air evincing an acquaintance with the world of letters and of art, such as only travel can produce.

He asked the name of his stranger guest, as Carson approaching addressed him, and at once commenced a conversation in English, saying with a look of satisfied pleasure, "I address you in your native tongue, which I presume is agreeable, though you speak very good Spanish;" to which Carson, much more surprised to hear his native language so fluently spoken, than his host was to be addressed in Spanish, replied,

"It is certainly agreeable to find you can give me the information which, as an American, I seek, in the language my mother taught me," and at once they were on terms of easy familiarity.

As it was early morning, his host asked Carson to take a cup of coffee with him, and conducting him to the breakfast room, presented him to the family—a wife and several grown sons and daughters.

Carson enjoyed the social part of this treat more than the tempting viands with which the board was loaded. Though Spanish was the language most used by the family, all spoke English, and a young man from Massachusetts was with them as a tutor to some of the younger children. Breakfast over, the host invited him to visit the vineyard, which he said was hardly in condition to be exhibited, as the picking had commenced two weeks before. He said his yard, of a thousand varas, yielded him more grapes than he could manage to dispose of, though last year he had made several butts of wine, and dried five thousand pounds of raisins. The vines were in the form of little trees, so closely had they been trimmed, and were still loaded with the purple clusters. Tasting them, Carson justly remarked that he had never eaten so good a grape.

"No," said his host, "I think not; neither have I, though I have traveled through Europe. The valley of the Rhine, nor of the Tagus, produces anywhere a grape like ours. I think that the Los Angeles grape is fit food indeed for angels—is quite equal to the grapes of Eshcol—

you remember the heavy clusters that were found there, so that two men carried one between them on a pole resting upon their shoulders. See that now," and he drew Carson to a vine whose trunk was six inches through, and yet it needed a prop to sustain the weight of the two clusters of grapes it bore.

A species of the cactus, called the prickly pear, enclosed the vineyard, and this really bore pears, or a fruit of light orange color, in the form of a pear, but covered with a down of prickles. The Indian boy brought a towel, and wiping the fruit until it shone, gave to Carson to taste. It was sweetish, juicy, and rich, but with less of flavor than a pear. Beyond the vineyard were groves of fig and orange trees. The figs were hardly ripe, being the third crop of the season, while the oranges were nearly fit for picking. The host said that his oranges were better than usual this season, but he did not know what he should do with them. He was in the habit of shipping them to Santa Barbara and Monterey, and thence taking some to San Jose; but latterly oranges had been brought to Monterey from the Sandwich Islands by ships in the service of the Hudson Bay Company, returning from the China trade to the mouth of the Columbia, which, arriving before his were ripe, he found the fruit market forestalled.

"This is the finest country the sun shines upon," said he, "and we can live luxuriously upon just what will grow on our own farms; but we cannot get rich. Our cattle will only bring the value of the hides; our horses are of little value, for there are plenty running wild which good huntsmen can take with the lasso; and, as for fruit, from which I had hoped to realize something, the market is cut off by Yankee competition. I think we shall have the Americans with us before many years, and for my part I hope we shall. The idea of Californians generally, as well as of other Mexicans, that they are too shrewd for them, is true enough; but certainly there is plenty of room for a large population, and I should prefer that the race that has most enterprise, should come and cultivate the country with us."

Carson's youth commanded him to listen, rather than to advance his own sentiments; but he expressed his pleasure at hearing his host compliment the Americans, and said in reply, "I have not been an extensive traveler, and have chosen the life of a mountaineer, for a time certainly; but since I came to California, I am half inclined to decide to make this my home when I get tired of trapping. I like the hunt, and have found game exceedingly plenty here, but there is no buffalo, and I want that. Give me buffalo, and I would settle in California."

He described to his host a buffalo hunt in which he engaged with the Sioux Indians, before he left his father's home, at fifteen years of age, and another later, since he came into the mountains. He had hunted buffalo every year since he was twelve years old.

The Don was charmed with the earnestness and the frankness, and manifest integrity of the youth, and turning his glance upon him, with the slightly quizzical expression the face a Spaniard so readily assumes, he inquired how many buffalo he had ever killed.

"Not so many as I have deer, because I was always in a deer country; but in the eight years since I commenced going in the buffalo ranges, I must have killed five hundred. The hunter does not kill without he wishes to use. I was often permitted to take a shot at the animals before I was able to help in dressing them."

But Carson felt it might seem like boasting,

for him to tell his own exploits, and changing the theme, remarked,

"Your horses would make excellent buffalo hunters, with the proper training, and I have some at camp that I intend shall see buffalo. But why do you not deal gently with them when they are first caught, and keep the fire they have in the herd? Pardon me, but I think in taming your horses, you break their spirits."

"My tutor has said the same, and I too have thought so in regard to the Mexican style of training our horses. We mount one just caught from the drove, and ride him till he becomes gentle from exhaustion. The French do not train horses in that way, nor the English; I have not been in the United States. Our custom is brought from Spain; and it answers well enough with us, where our horses go in droves, and when one is used up, we turn him out and take up another; but when we take this animal again, he is just as wild as at the first; we can not afford to spend time on breaking him when it must be done over again directly."

And so the two hours, which Carson had allotted for his visit, passed in easy chat, and when he took his leave, his host expressed his thanks for his visit, and promised to return it at the camp.

Carson did not again see his courteous host, for early on the following morning, Mr. Young found it necessary that he should get his men away from Los Angeles as speedily as possible. They had been indulging to excess in bad liquors, and having none of the best feelings towards the Mexicans, many quarrels, some ending in bloodshed, had ensued.

He therefore despatched Carson ahead with a few men, promising to follow and overtake him at the earliest moment, and waiting another day, he managed to get his followers in a tolerably sober condition, and succeeded, though not without much trouble, in getting away without the loss of a man, though the Mexicans were desperately enraged at the death of one of their townsmen, who had been killed in a chance fray. In three days he overtook Carson, and the party, once more reunited, advanced rapidly towards the Colorado River, his men working with a heartiness and cheerfulness, resulting from a consciousness of their misconduct at Los Angeles, which, but for the prudent discretion of Young and Carson, might have resulted disastrously to all concerned.

In nine days they were ready to commence trapping on the Colorado, and in a short time added here to the large stock of furs they had brought from California.

Here while left in charge of the camp, with only a few men, Carson found himself suddenly confronted by several hundred Indians. They entered the camp with the utmost assurance, and acted as though they felt the power of their numbers. Carson at once suspected that all was not right, and attempting to talk with them, he soon discovered that, with all their *sang-froid*, each of them carried his weapons concealed beneath his garments, and immediately ordered them out of camp. Seeing the small number of the white men, the Indians were not inclined to obey, but chose to wait their time and do as they pleased, as they were accustomed to do with the Mexicans. They soon learned that they were dealing with men of different mettle, for Carson was a man not to be trifled with.

His men stood around him, each with his rifle resting in the hollow of the arm, ready to be dropped to deadly aim on the sign from their young commander. Carson addressed the old chief in Spanish (for he had betrayed his knowledge of that language), and warned him that though they were few, they were determined to sell their lives dearly. The Indians awed, it would seem, by the bold and defiant language of Carson, and finding that any plunder they might acquire, would be purchased at a heavy sacrifice sullenly withdrew, and left the party to pursue their journey unmolested.

Any appearance of fear would have cost the lives of Carson and probably of the whole party, but the Indian warriors were too chary of their lives to rush into death's door unprovoked, even for the sake of the rich plunder they might hope to secure. Carson's cool bravery saved the trappers and all their effects; and this first command in an Indian engagement is but a picture of his conduct in a hundred others, when the battles were with weapons other than the tongue. The intention of the Indians had been to drive away the animals, first causing a stampede, when they would become lawful plunder, but they dared not undertake it.

The wily craftiness of the Indians induced the necessity for constant vigilance against them, and in the school this youth had been in all his life, he had shown himself an apt scholar

CHAPTER VIII.

WHILE on the Colorado, Young's party discovered a company of Indians (with whom they had had a previous skirmish), as they were coming out from Los Angeles, and charging suddenly among them, succeeded in taking a large herd of cattle from them in the Indians' own style. The same week an Indian party came past their camp in the night, with a drove of a hundred horses, evidently just stolen from a Mexican town in Sonora. The trappers, with their guns for their pillows, were ready in an instant for the onslaught, and captured these horses also, the Indians hurrying away for fear of the deadly rifle. The next day they selected such as they wanted from the herd, choosing of course the finest, and turning the rest loose, to be taken again by the Indians, or to become the wild mustangs that roamed the plains of Northern Mexico, in droves of tens of thousands, and which could be captured and tamed only by the use of the lasso.

Mr. Young and his party trapped down the Colorado and up the Gila with success, then crossed to the vicinity of the New Mexican copper mines, where they left their furs and went to Santa Fé. Having procured their license to trade with the Indians about the copper mines, they returned thither for their furs, went back to Santa Fé and disposed of them to great advantage. The party disbanded with several hundred dollars apiece, which most of them expended as sailors do their earnings when they come into port. Of course Carson was hail fellow well met with them for a time. He had not hitherto taken the lesson that all have to learn, viz., that the ways of pleasure are deceitful paths; and to resist temptation needs a large amount of courage—larger perhaps than to encounter any physical danger; at least the moral courage it requires is of a higher tone than the physical courage which would carry one through a fight with a grizzly bear triumphantly; that the latter assists the former; indeed that the highest moral courage must be aided by physical bravery, but that the latter may exist entirely independently of the former.

Carson learned during this season of hilarity

the necessity of saying No ! and he did so persistently, knowing that if he failed in this he would be lost to himself and to everything dear in life. He was now twenty-one, and though the terrible ordeal of poverty had been nobly borne, and he had conquered, the latter ordeal of temptation from the sudden possession of what was to him a large sum of money, had proved, for once, too much. And it is well for him perhaps it was so ; as it enabled him to sow his wild oats in early youth.

It is not improbable that some of this party belonged to the class of Canadians called *coureurs des bois*, whose habits Mr. Irving thus describes in his Astoria :

" A new and anomalous class of men gradually grew out of this trade. These were called *coureurs des bois*, rangers of the woods ; originally men who had accompanied the Indians in their hunting expeditions, and made themselves acquainted with remote tracts and tribes ; and who now became, as it were, pedlers of the wilderness. These men would set out from Montreal with canoes well stocked with goods, with arms and ammunition, and would make their way up the mazy and wandering rivers that interlace the vast forests of the Canadas, coasting

the most remote lakes, and creating new wants
and habitudes among the natives. Sometimes
they sojourned for months among them, assimilating to their tastes and habits with the happy
facility of Frenchmen; adopting in some degree
the Indian dress, and not unfrequently taking
to themselves Indian wives.

"Twelve, fifteen, eighteen months would often
elapse without any tidings of them, when they
would come sweeping their way down the Ottawa in full glee, their canoes laden down with
packs of beaver skins. Now came their turn
for revelry and extravagance. 'You would be
amazed,' says an old writer already quoted,
'if you saw how lewd these pedlers are when
they return; how they feast and game, and
how prodigal they are, not only in their clothes,
but upon their sweethearts. Such of them as
are married have the wisdom to retire to their
own houses; but the bachelors do just as an
East Indiaman and pirates are wont to do; for
they lavish, eat, drink, and play all away as
long as the goods hold out; and when these
are gone, they even sell their embroidery, their
lace, and their clothes. This done, they are
forced upon a new voyage for subsistence."

Many of these *coureurs des bois* became so

accustomed to the Indian mode of living, and the perfect freedom of the wilderness, that they lost all relish for civilization, and identified themselves with the savages among whom they dwelt, or could only be distinguished from them by superior licentiousness.

In the autumn Carson joined another trapping party under Mr. Fitzpatrick, whom we shall have frequent occasion to mention hereafter. They proceeded up the Platte and Sweet Water past Goose Creek to the Salmon River, where they wintered, like other parties, sharing the good will of the Nez Perces Indians, and having the vexations of the Blackfeet for a constant fear. Mr. Fitzpatrick, less daring than Carson, declined sending him to punish this tribe for their depredations.

In the spring they came to Bear River, which flows from the north to Salt Lake. Carson and four men left Mr. Fitzpatrick here, and went ten days to find Captain Gaunt in the place called the New Park, on the head waters of the Arkansas, where they spent the trapping season, and wintered. While the party were wintering in camp, being robbed of some of their horses by a band of sixty Crow Indians, Carson, as usual, was appointed to lead the party sent in pursuit of the plunderers. With only twelve men he took up the trail, came upon the Indians in one of their strongholds, cut loose the animals, which were tied within ten feet of the fort of logs in which the enemy had taken shelter, attacked them, killed five of their warriors, and made good his retreat with the recovered horses; an Indian of another tribe who was with the trappers bringing away a Crow scalp as a trophy.*

In the spring, while trapping on the Platte River, two men belonging to the party deserted and robbed a *cache*, or underground deposit of furs, which had been made by Captain Gaunt in the neighborhood. Carson, with only one companion, went off in pursuit of the thieves, who, however, were never heard of afterwards.

Not finding the plunderers, Carson and his companion remained at the old camp on the Arkansas, where the *cache* had been made, until they were relieved by a party sent out from the United States with supplies for Captain Gaunt's trappers. They were soon after joined by a party of Gaunt's men, and started to his camp. On their way they had repeated encounters with Indians attempting to steal their horses, but easily beat them off and saved their property.

* Cutts. Conquest of California and New Mexico.

On one occasion when Carson and the other trappers were out in search of *beaver sign*, they came suddenly upon a band of sixty warriors well armed and mounted. In the presence of such a force their only safety was in flight. Amid a shower of bullets from the Indian rifles, they made good their escape. Carson considered this one of his narrowest escapes.

CHAPTER IX.

In the spring of 1832, Mr. Gaunt's party had been unsuccessful, and were now upon a stream where there was no beaver, therefore Carson announced his intention of hunting on his own account. Two of his companions joined him, and the three for the whole season pursued their work successfully, high up in the mountain streams, while the Indians were down in the plains hunting buffalo; and taking their fur to Taos, disposed of them at a remunerative price. While the two former spent their money in the usual way, Carson saved his hard earnings which his companions were so recklessly throwing away. This self-discipline, and schooling himself to virtue and temperance, was not without effort on the part of Kit Carson, for he loved the good will and kindly civilities of his companions; but he knew also that he could not have his cake and eat it too, and chose to save his money and his strength for future use.

While remaining at Taos, Captain Lee, formerly of the United States army, now a partner of Bent and St. Vrain, at Bent's Fort, invited Carson to join an expedition which he was arranging. Carson accepted his offer, starting in October. Going northward they came up with a party of twenty traders and trappers, upon a branch of the Green River, and all entered winter quarters here together.

Mr. Robideau had in his employ a Californian Indian, very skilful in the chase—whether for game or for human prey—very courageous, and able to endure the greatest hardships and whose conduct hitherto had won the confidence of all. This Indian had left clandestinely, taking with him six of Mr. Robideau's most valuable horses, which were worth at least twelve hundred dollars. Mr. Robideau, determined to recover them if possible, solicited Carson to pursue and overtake the Indian. Kit asked his employer, Mr Lee's, permission to serve Mr. Robideau, which was readily granted, when he at once prepared himself for hard riding and sturdy resistance.

From a Utah village near he obtained an intelligent and brave young warrior to join him—

for Carson's reputation for courage, skill, and efficiency, were known to the tribes, and many of its braves were attached to him, and afterwards proved that they cherished a lasting friendship for him.

For a time the blindness of the trail compelled them to go slowly, but once sure of its direction, they pursued it with the utmost speed down Green River, Carson concluding the Indian was directing his course toward California. When they had gone a hundred miles on their way, the Indian's horse was suddenly taken sick. The Indian would not consent to continue the pursuit, as Carson suggested, on foot, and he therefore determined to go on alone, and putting spurs to his horse resolved not to return until he had succeeded in recovering Mr. Robideau's property. With practised eye ever upon the trail, he revolved in his mind the expert skill he might need to exercise in encountering the wily savage. This desperate expedition Carson had boldly entered into, not with rashness, but he had accepted it as an occasion that demanded the hazard. At the distance of thirty miles from where he left his Utah companion, he discovered the object of his chase. The Indian too had discovered him, and to pre pare himself for the attack, turned to seek a shelter whence he might fire and reload without exposure to the shot from Carson's rifle—which he had unslung when first he discovered the Indian.

With his horse at full speed at the moment the Indian reached his cover, Carson fired with aim so true that the Indian gave one bound and fell dead beside his horse, while his gun went off at the same instant. No further particulars of description or speculation can add to the interest of this picture. We leave it to the imagination of the reader, as an illustration of the daring and fidelity of Kit Carson. Collecting the horses, he soon had the pleasure, after a few minor difficulties of presenting to Mr. Robideau the six animals he had lost, in as good condition as when they were stolen, and of announcing to him the fact that there lived one less rogue.

Soon after Carson's return to camp some trappers brought them news that Messrs. Fitzpatrick and Bridger were camped fifteen miles from them. Captain Lee and Carson at once concluded that to them they might sell their goods. They started for their camp and were as successful as they had hoped, for they sold their whole stock of goods to this party, and took their pay in furs. Their contract being now completed, Carson joined Mr. Fitzpatrick again in a trapping expedition, but did not remain long with him, because the party was too large to make it pay, or even to work harmoniously together. With three men whom he chose from the many who wished to join him, Carson again commenced trapping on his own account. They trapped all summer on the Laramie, with unusual success. It was while Carson was out on this trap that he had the adventure with the grizzly bears,[*] which he considered the most perilous that he ever passed through. He had gone out from the camp on foot to shoot game for supper, and had just brought down an elk, when two grizzly bears came suddenly upon him. His rifle being empty, there was no way of escape from instant death but to run with his utmost speed for the nearest tree. He reached a sapling with the bears just at his heels. Cutting off a limb of the tree with his knife, he used that as his only weapon of defense. When the bears climbed so as nearly to reach him, he gave them smart raps on the nose, which sent

[*] Peters.

them away growling; but when the pain ceased they would return again only to have the raps repeated. In this way nearly the whole night was spent, when finally the bears became discouraged, and retired from the contest. Waiting until they were well out of sight, Carson descended from his unenviable position, and made the best of his way into camp, which he reached about daylight. The elk had been devoured by wolves before it could be found, and his three companions were only too glad to see him, to be troubled about breakfasting on beaver, as they had supped the night before; for trappers in camp engaged in their business had this resort for food when all others failed.

Laramie River flows into the North Platte, upon the south side. The country through which it flows is open, yet the stream is bordered with a variety of shrubbery, and in many spots the cottonwood grows luxuriantly, and for this reason the locality is favorable for the grizzly bear.

Baird says of this bear: "While the black bear is the bear of the forest, the grizzly is the bear of the chapparal, the latter choosing an open country, whether plain or mountain, whose surface is covered with dense thickets of manzanita or shrub oak, which furnish him with his favorite food, and clumps of service bushes, and low cherry; and whose streams are lined with tangled thickets of low grape vine and wild plumb." The grizzly is not so good at climbing as the black bear, and can best manage by resting upon his haunches and mounting with his fore arms upon the bushes that he cannot pull over, to gather the berries, of which he is very fond.

"Only in a condition of hunger will he attack a man unprovoked, but when he does, the energy with which he fights, prevents the Indians from seeking the sport of a hunt for the grizzly bear. He is monarch of the plain, with only their opposition, and has departed only before the rifle of the white hunter. An Indian, who would, alone, undertake to conquer a dozen braves of another tribe, would shrink from attacking a grizzly bear; and to have killed one, furnishes a story for a lifetime, and gives a reputation that descends to posterity. The mounted hunter can rarely bring his horse to approach him near enough for a shot."

Soon after his encounter with the bears, Carson and his men were rejoiced by the arrival of

Captain Bridger, so long a mountaineer of note, and with him his whole band. Carson and his three companions joined with them and were safe; and now for the first time he attended the summer rendezvous of trappers on the Green River, where they assembled for the disposal of their furs, and the purchase of such outfit as they needed.

Carson for the Fall hunt joined a company of fifty, and went to the country of the Blackfeet at the head waters of the Missouri; but the Indians were so numerous, and so determined upon hostility, that a white man could not leave his camp without danger of being shot down; therefore, quitting the Blackfeet country, they camped on the Big Snake River for winter quarters.

During the winter months, the Blackfeet had in the night run off eighteen of their horses, and Kit Carson, with eleven men, was sent to recover them, and chastise their temerity. They rode fifty miles through the snow before coming up with the Indians, and instantly made an attempt to recover their animals, which were loose and quietly grazing.

The Indians, wearing snow shoes, had the advantage, and Carson readily granted the parley they asked. One man from each party advanced, and between the contending ranks had a talk. The Indians informed them that they supposed they had been robbing the Snake Indians, and did not desire to steal from white men. Of course this tale was false, and Carson asked why they did not lay down their arms and ask for a smoke, but to this they had no reply to make. However, both parties laid aside their weapons and prepared for the smoke; and the lighted calumet was puffed by every one of the savages and the whites alternately, and the head men of the savages made several long non-committal speeches, to which, in reply, the trappers came directly to the point, and said they would hear nothing of conciliation from them until their property was returned.

After much talk, the Indians brought in five of the poorest horses. The whites at once started for their guns, which the Indians did at the same time, and the fight at once commenced. Carson and a comrade named Markland having seized their rifles first, were at the lead, and selected for their mark two Indians who were near each other and behind different trees; but as Kit was about to fire, he perceived Markland's antagonist aiming at him with death-like precision, while Markland had not noticed him, and on the instant, neglecting his own adversary, he sent a bullet through the heart of the other savage, but at the moment saw that his own enemy's rifle was aimed at his breast. He was not quite quick enough to dodge the ball, and it struck the side of his neck, and passed through his shoulder, shattering the bone.

Carson was thenceforward only a spectator of the fight, which continued until night, when both parties retired from the field of battle and went into camp.

Carson's wound was very painful, and bled freely, till the cold checked the flow of blood. They dared not light a fire, and in the cold and darkness, Carson uttered not a word of complaint, nor did even a groan escape him. His companions were earnest in their sympathy but he was too brave to need it, or to allow his wound to influence the course they should pursue. In a council of war which they held, it was decided that, as they had slain several Indians, and had themselves only one wounded, they had best return to camp, as they were in unfit condition to continue the pursuit. Arriving at camp, another council was held, at which it was decided to send thirty men under Captain

Bridger, to pursue and chastise these Blackfeet thieves. This party followed the Indian trail several days, but finally returned, concluding it was useless to search further, as they had failed to overtake them.

6

CHAPTER X

THE Spring hunt opened on the Green River, and continuing there a while, the party went to the Big Snake; and after trapping with extraordinary success for a few weeks, returned to the Summer rendezvous, held again upon the Green River. Meantime Carson had recovered from his wound.

An unusually large number of trappers and traders, with great numbers from the neighboring Indian tribes, assembled at this rendezvous, made up of Canadians, Frenchmen, Dutchmen, Spaniards, and many a backwoodsman, who had lived upon the borders, perhaps, for three generations, removing when a neighbor came within ten miles, because *near* neighbors were a nuisance to him. Let us see the parties as they come in, the leader, or the one to whom fitness accords this position, having selected the spot for the camp, so remote from every other, as to have plenty of grass about it for the animals of the party. Perhaps a tent is spread, at least, everything is put in proper order, according to the notions and the tastes of the men who make up the party; for the camp is the home of its members, and here they will receive visitors, and exchange courtesies.

The party or parties that have made the special arrangements for the rendezvous—traders with a full supply of goods—have spread a large tent in a central spot of the general encampment, where the whole company, save those detained at each camp in charge of the animals belonging to it, will assemble, at certain hours each day, the time upon which the sales are announced to take place, and the exchanges commence.

The several parties arriving first, have been obliged to wait until all expected for the season have arrived, because there is a feeling of honor as well as a care for competition, that compels the custom. The traders take furs or money for their goods, which bring prices that seem fabulous to those unaccustomed to the sight or stories of mountain life. The charge, of course, is made upon the ground of the expense and risk of bringing goods eight hundred and a thousand miles into the wilderness, from the nearest points in western Missouri and St Louis.

Irving opens his Astoria with the following " Two leading objects of commercial gain have given birth to wide daring and enterprise in the early history of the Americas: the precious metals of the South and the rich peltries of the North." When he wrote this, it was true of the localities he named—the gold was not yet an attraction, except in the south, and only the British Fur Company in Canada had become an object of history in this branch of trade. He says, " While the fiery and magnificent Spaniard influenced with the mania for gold, has extended his discoveries and conquests over those brilliant countries, scorched by the ardent sun of the tropics, the adroit Frenchman, and the cool and calculating Briton, have pursued the less splendid, but no less lucrative, traffic in furs, amidst the hyperborean regions of the Canadas, until they advanced even within the Arctic Circle.

" These two pursuits have thus, in a manner been the pioneers and precursors of civilization. Without pausing on the borders, they have penetrated at once, in defiance of difficulties and dangers, to the heart of savage countries; laying open the hidden secrets of the wilderness; leading the way to remote regions of beauty and fertility, that might have remained unexplored for ages, and beckoning after them the slow and pausing steps of agriculture and civilization. It was the fur trade, in fact, that gave early sustenance and vitality to the great Canadian provinces.

"Being destitute of the precious metals, they were for a long time neglected by the parent country. The French adventurers, however, who had settled on the banks of the St. Lawrence, soon found that in the rich peltries of the interior, they had sources of wealth that might almost rival the mines of Mexico and Peru. The Indians, as yet unacquainted with the artificial value given to some descriptions of furs, in civilized life, brought quantities of the most precious kinds and bartered them away for European trinkets and cheap commodities. Immense profits were thus made by the early traders, and the traffic was pursued with avidity.

"As the valuable furs became scarce in the neighborhood of the settlements, the Indians of the vicinity were stimulated to take a wider range in their hunting expeditions; they were generally accompanied on these expeditions by some of the traders or their dependants, who shared in the toils and perils of the chase, and at the same time, made themselves acquainted with the best hunting grounds, and with the remote tribes whom they encouraged to bring peltries to the settlements. In this way the trade augmented, and was drawn from remote quarters to Montreal. Every now and then a large body of Ottawas, Hurons, and other tribes who hunted the countries bordering on the great lakes, would come down in a squadron of light canoes, laden with beaver skins and other spoils of the year's hunting. The canoes would be unladen, taken on shore, and their contents disposed in order. A camp of birch bark would be pitched outside of the town, and a kind of primitive fair opened with that grave ceremonial so dear to the Indians.

" Now would ensue a brisk traffic with the merchants, and all Montreal would be alive with naked Indians, running from shop to shop, bargaining for arms, kettles, knives, axes, blankets, bright-colored cloths, and other articles of use or fancy ; upon all which, the merchants were sure to clear two hundred per cent.

" Their wants and caprices being supplied, they would take leave, strike their tents, launch their canoes, and ply their way up the Ottawa to the lakes."

Later, the French traders, *coureurs des bois*, penetrated the remote forests, carrying such goods as the Indians required, and held rendezvous among them, on a smaller scale, but similar to the one Carson had attended, so far as the Indian trade was concerned. But the Yankee element of character preponderated among the traders and trappers from the States; besides the greater difficulty and expense necessarily incurred to reach the hunting grounds by land than in canoe, called into the work only men of energy and higher skill than the employees, mostly French, in the service of the Hudson Bay Fur Company, and a score of smaller parties, each owning no authority outside itself, adopted the plan of these summer encampments, during the season when the fur of the beaver and the otter was not good, as an arrangement for mutual convenience; and the Indians of this more southern section availed themselves of the occasion, for their own pleasure and profit, and to the advantage and satisfaction of the traders, whose prices ruled high in proportion to the difficulty of transit, as well as the monopoly in their hands of the articles deemed necessary to the trapper's dress, culinary establishment, and outfit. These consisted of a woolen shirt, a sash or belt, and with some stockings, coffee, and black pepper, and salt, unless he could supply himself from the licks the buffalo visits; with tin kettle, and cup, and frying pan; the accouterments of the horse, saddle and pack-saddle, bridle, spurs, and horseshoes; with material for bait; and last, but not least, tobacco, which, if he did not use, he carried to give to the Indians—made up not only the necessaries, but the luxuries, which the Indian and the white man indulged in, and for which, at such times, they paid their money or their furs.

Perhaps the trapper took an Indian wife, and then she must be made fine with dress, denoting the dignity of her position as wife of a white man, and presents must be given to the friends of his bride. This was usually an expensive luxury, but indulged in most frequently by the French and Canadian trappers, many of whom are now living quietly upon their farms in Oregon and California, and the numerous valleys of the West. Indeed we might give the names of many a mountain ranger, and pioneer of note, first a trapper, who still lives surrounded by his Indian wife and their children, and finds himself thus connected with this people, having their utmost confidence, chosen the chief of his tribe, and able to care for them as no one not in such association could.

At almost any point upon Green River the grass upon the bottom lands is sufficient for a night's encampment for a small party; but at the place selected for the rendezvous, in the space of two or three miles upon either side of the river, the bottom spreads out in a broad prairie, and the luxuriant growth of grass, with the country open all about it, made the spot desirable for a large encampment.

CHAPTER XI.

EARLY in the summer the grass is green, but later it is hay made naturally, root and branch dried on the ground—there is no sod—and this, though less agreeable, is more nutritious for the animals than fresh grass.

A scattered growth of fine old trees furnishes shade at every camp, and immediately about the great tent they afford protection from the sun to parties of card-players, or a "Grocery stand," at which the principal article of sale is "whisky by the glass;" and perhaps, further on is a *monte* table, parties from several Indian tribes, and the pioneer of semi-civilization—the backwoodsman—has come in "with his traps," a few bags of flour, and possibly some cheese and butter, and the never failing cask of whisky. Perhaps his wagon is the grocery stand, to which we have just alluded. Without extenuation, these encampments were grand occasions of which a few descriptions may be found written at the time by men of science and in tellectual culture, like Sir Wm. Stewart, who traveled upon these plains for pleasure, or the Rev. Samuel Parker, who happened at a Green River rendezvous, in 1835, while on his way to the Columbia River, under the auspices of the American Board of Commissioners for Foreign Missions. This was long before Brigham Young came West—before his scheme of religious colonization had its birth.

There is now—has been for years—a trading post, where a Canadian Frenchman and an American partner with Indian wives, have provided entertainment or furnished supplies to emigrants and Indians. It is near the Green River crossing, on the road from the South Pass to great Salt Lake City, via Fort Bridger.

Amid the motley company it might be expected that quarrels would arise, and disorderly conduct, growing out of the feuds among the tribes of Indians. These were kept in abeyance as much as possible, and already Carson's popularity with them enabled him to act the part of peacemaker between them and the quarrelsome whites, as well as between each other, for many of them recognized him as the brave who had led excursions, whose success they had felt and suffered, and even though leader of victorious parties against themselves, they admired his prowess still; for the party of Blackfeet came to the rendezvous under the protection of the white flag, and for the time, no one more truly buried the hatchet than Carson, though just recovered from a wound given by a party of that tribe, which had nearly cost him his life, and of which we have written in a previous chapter.

There was belonging to one of the trapping parties a Frenchman by the name of Shuman, known at the rendezvous as "the big bully of the mountains," exceedingly annoying on account of his boasts and taunts, a constant exciter of tumult and disorder, especially among the Indians. Bad enough at any time, with the means now for intoxication, he was even more dangerous.

The habits of the mountaineers, without law save such as the exigency of the moment demanded, required a firm, steady hand to rule. Carson had feared the results of this man's lawlessness, and had often desired to be rid of him, but he had not as yet found the proper opportunity. The mischiefs he committed grew worse and worse, and yet for the sake of peace they were borne unresistingly At length an op portunity offered to try his courage. One day Shuman, boasting of his exploits, was particularly insolent and insulting towards all Americans, whom he described as only fit to be whipped with switches. Carson was in the crowd, and immediately stepped forward, saying, "I am an American, the most inconsiderable one among them, but if you wish to die, I will accept your challenge."

Shuman defied him. He was sitting upon his horse, with his loaded rifle in his hand. Carson leaped upon his horse with a loaded pistol, and both rushed into close combat. They fired, almost at the same moment, but Carson an instant before his boasting antagonist. Their horses' heads touched, Shuman's ball just grazing Carson's cheek, near the left eye, and cutting off some locks of his hair. Carson's ball entered Shuman's hand, came out at the wrist, and passed through his arm above the elbow. The bully begged for his life, and it was spared; and from that time forward, Americans were no more insulted by him.

If, as in other duels, we were to go back to remoter causes, and find in this too, the defense of woman—a Blackfoot beauty—whom Shuman had determined to abuse, which Carson's interference only had prevented, for the sake of truth, of honor, and virtue, as against insolence, falsehood, and treachery, although the girl did belong to a tribe that was treacherous; we shall be but giving a point to the story that it needs for completeness, and show Carson in the exalted manliness and fidelity of his character.

The trappers made arrangements at the rendezvous for the fall hunt; and the party who were so fortunate as to secure Carson's services, went to the Yellowstone River, in the Blackfeet country, but met with no success. Crossing through the Crows' country to the Big Horn River, they met the party of Blackfeet returning from Green River. Carson held a parley with them, as was his custom whenever it was safe to go to an Indian camp. He told them he had seen none of their people, and that the tomahawk was buried if they were faithful to him. "But," said he, "the Crows are my friends, and while I am with them, they must be yours."

On the Big Horn, too, their success was no better, and Carson did not meet his Crow friends. On the Big Snake, too, which they next visited, the result was the same.

They here met a party from the Hudson

Bay Company, led by a Mr. McCoy. Carson and five of his companions accepted the offer he made them, and went with him to the Humboldt River, trapping with little success from its source to the desert where it loses itself, and where the termini of several other large rivers are all within a day's ride, according to the statement of residents at this point. Captain McCoy said to Carson, as he and two of the company started off upon the desert,

"Do not be gone longer than to-morrow night, and if you strike a stream where there is beaver—there must be water between here and those snow mountains—we will trap a few days longer."

On they rode over the artemisia plain till the lake was out of view from an eminence which Carson climbed; then struck a tract of country entirely destitute of every sign of animal or vegetable life, with surface as smooth as the floor for miles in extent, then broken by a ridge a few feet high, like the rim to a lake, whose bottom they had passed, to plunge immediately upon another like it, with perhaps a white and glistening crystallization spread thinly over it.

Carson knew he must be upon the celebrated

Mud Lakes of which he had heard, and of which he had seen miniature specimens further east. Over these lake bottoms of earth, that broken, seemed like mingled sand and ashes, but which bore the tread of their horses, and over which they seemed to fly rather than to step, so fragrant and exhilarating was the atmosphere, they traveled thirty miles, then struck the artemisia plains again, only there was less of even this worthless production for the next ten miles than he had seen before for a long distance.

Through a heavy sand the weary horses plod, for they had come forty or fifty miles beneath a burning sun without food and without water. On they ride, for rest and refreshment to themselves was not to be thought of till they have it for the animals. The river is gained! a broad, deep current of water, muddy like that of the Platte, supplies the moisture to the trees, whose tops ascend only a few feet above the desert level, and whose trunks rise from green meadows but little above the surface of the water. The bottom lands are narrow, and the abrupt bank descends to the water perpendicularly twenty feet or more, seemingly of clayey earth, so soft, the water constantly wore upon it, and evidently the river channel was settling, as the years advanced. There were no signs of beaver, and, from the nature of the banks, there would be none, unless high up on the stream.

7

CHAPTER XII.

CAPTAIN McCoy had calculated that he would soon find game in the country through which his route lay, and therefore he had turned over to Carson, and the division of the party under his command, nearly all the food which was left, but this was insufficient to give them full meals for more than three days. Their prospect was a dreary one indeed, for at the earlier season of coming down the river, they had not half enough to eat, even with the few beaver they had taken, to add to the supply, and even this was now denied them. And now, that the reader may understand Carson's position, we invite him to enjoy with us a few of the incidents passed through, and views observed in our passage up this river, which the untraveled eastern man would find so entirely new, and the man of travel and of letters would find so full of interest, as did the man whose name the river bears, for it was named by Fremont, after Carson, whom he had learned to love and respect, long before he reached it. We shall speak especially of the features of this country, common to so much that lies between the civilizations of the Atlantic and the Pacific slopes, though the latter was not a civilization; and when from the desert Carson gazed with admiration at the snow mountains, he surmised, as he afterwards realized through hunger, cold, danger, and suffering, that this was the chain of mountains which separated him from California.

At the station-house, upon the lake, called the sink of the Humboldt, we were told that the Humboldt did not connect with this lake except in the spring season, after the rains, and that for the last two years it had not been connected even at that time; and that in the autumn one could pass, between the lake and the limit of the marsh in which the river loses itself, upon dry ground; and that the sinks, or the margins of the lakes or marshes in which the Carson, the Walker, and the Susan Rivers, neither of them less than a hundred miles in length, and some of them several hundred, in the wet season empty or lose themselves, were all within the limit of a single day's ride, and in the direct vicinity of the desert upon which the reader last saw Carson.

It was the evening of the second of July, during a rain storm, (an unusual occurrence at this season of the year, no traveler having ever reported a similar one so far as we had heard,) that, weary, and wet, and cold, we found our way in the dark to this river in the wilderness. The house of the traders at the sink was made of logs, with two rooms—the logs having been drawn from the mountains, forty miles distant. There was no timber in sight, and nothing that was green except some grass about the lake, which we were told was poison, and on examining, we found it encrusted with a crystallization of potash, left on it by the subsiding water in which the grass had started.

During the wet season, the water of the lake overflows its banks, and the banks of the river are also overflowed, while the water standing upon the surface of the ground is strongly impregnated with potash, not only near the sink, but far up the stream, nearly to its source, the same cause existing, though only in occasional spots is it exhibited to the same degree as about the lake. It is not improbable that some immense coal formation might have been consumed here in some remote past age, though that is a matter for more scientific examination than becomes this work.

But, to leave speculation; the occupants of the station, whilom trappers in the mountains, furnished barley for our animals, and we might have purchased coffee, or a rusty gun, or bad whisky, but little else, for their regular supplies for the emigrants, who were soon expected to arrive, had not yet come in. The parties bound east had passed, and the Mormons, with their herds of cattle for the California markets, had been met beyond the desert. A party of Pah Utah or Piete Indians, a tribe of Diggers, were hanging about the encampment, and possibly had caused the stampede of the Mormon oxen, which one of their herdsmen had reported to us as occurring here. The traders on the plains are charged with conniving at such expeditions of the Indians, and of sharing with them the plunder. These traders may not have been privy to anything of the kind, but certain it is they always stood ready to purchase the worn-out stock of the overland emigrants, much of which is worthless to cross the desert, after the prior fifteen hundred miles of travel.

This is made a lucrative business, as will be readily imagined, when the number of animals driven over is taken into consideration, which has amounted to a hundred thousand annually, by this route, during several of the years since the quest for gold.

The traders said they had twenty-five hundred horses and as many oxen, in charge of herdsmen in the mountain valley. Shrewd men they were, one of them with an eye we would not warrant to look out from a kindly soul.

Miserable wretches were these Humboldt Diggers, with scarcely a trace of humanity in their composition, for they have not improved since Carson first met them, many years ago. The old chief was delighted with a lump of sugar, which one of our party gave him. He wore a long coat made of rabbit skins, warm and durable, strips of the skin with the hair out being wound around a deerskin thong, and these rolls woven into a garment, but the rest of the party were nearly naked.

Passing Lassen's meadows where the party lunched at a spring, indicated, as we approached, by a growth of willows, and striking upon the artemisia plain that constitutes the larger portion of the river valley, when about fifty miles from the station, we left the road by a blind trail, and approached the river, descending to the bottom land by a precipitous bluff thirty feet in height. The mountains approached close on the opposite side of the river, probably a mile distant, and enclosed us in a semicircle, while the bluff was lined with a scattered growth of alders.

It rained, was raining violently when we halted, and stretching a rope from alder to alder, with a blanket thrown over it, we thus made a tent, and established ourselves cosily to spend here the nation's Sabbath-day, the 4th of July.

The rain turned into snow towards evening, and covered the mountains to their base, but melting as it fell where we were encamped, and with the cooing of the doves which filled the alders, the croaking of the frogs in the marsh next the river, and the patter of the rain upon the bushes, we had other music—nature's deep bass—in a constant roaring sound, like that of old ocean at full tide on a sand beach of the open coast of the Pacific; or like the sound of Niagara, heard half a mile away, but there was no discoverable cause.

Going a mile up and down the river from the camp—if there is up and down to a dead river—we still heard the sound, the same in tone and power. Our Wyandotte—a member of the party who had crossed the plains with Col. Fremont—suggested that it was "the Humboldt sinking."

All the day of the 4th of July we rested here, with our animals in clover, amid the snow which reached even to the foot of the mountains opposite, and the dirge played for us by the unseen hand. It was a quiet, still sweetly sad day—pleasant in memory, and such an one as we shall never spend again—so far from civilized humanity, and in a place so remote from human footsteps, it seemed a natural wonder which had never been properly examined and explained.

Sooner than the old trappers anticipated, will the Humboldt be lined with farms, and the little mountain valleys filled with grazing herds, and the church spire and the cross upon an unassuming building in the center of a six-mile-square prairie, indicate the advance of civilization. Yet, except in the mud-lake localities, there is no tract of country that can well be more unpromising than that about the Humboldt; and not many years will elapse before science will make plain and palpable that wonder of the world, " the sinking of the Humboldt."

CHAPTER XIII.

THROUGH the country we have thus briefly described, Carson and his men had trapped, taking some small game, intending to return late in the season when the cold of this high altitude, with the sun low, was becoming terribly severe, while the grass was dead, and the birds of passage had all departed. Their prospects were cheerless and unpromising, nor were they at all improved after they left the Humboldt; for their route lay through an artemisia desert, varied only by an occasional little valley, where springs of water in the early season had induced the growth of grass.

On reaching Goose Creek, they found it frozen, so that there was no possibility of finding even roots, to satisfy their hunger. Though to-day this is the trail of California emigration, with plenty of grass, for a great portion of the way, in its season; now all was desolate, and inured as they were to hardship, Carson's men had never before suffered so much from hunger, nor did their animals fare much better. Captain McCoy had taken with him all not needed by Carson's party, because he could give them food, and it was fortunate for them he had adopted this course.

The magnificent mountain scenery on the route could scarcely excite admiration or remark from this company of hungry, toil-worn men ; even that unique exhibition of nature's improvised ideality, done in stone—pyramid circle—with its pagodas, temples, obelisks, and altars, within a curiously wrought rock wall, they only wished were the *adobe* walls and houses of Fort Hall. However, nothing daunted by the dreary prospect before them, they here bled their horses, and drank the precious draught, well knowing they were taking the wind from the sails upon which they must rely to waft them into port, if they ever reached it.

The next day, they were meditating the slaughter of one of their horses, when a party of Snake Indians fortunately came in sight. They had been out on the war trail, and returning, had little food, but Carson managed to purchase a fat horse, which they killed at once, and thus managed to live luxuriously till they reached the fort, able now to walk and give the horses the advantage of their diet.

Epicureans of civilization, when the squeamishness of an appetite, perverted by too delicate fare, is invited to such a repast, may rest assured that they know not the satisfaction such fare afforded to Kit Carson and his party. Horse beef was sweeter food to these starving men, than epicures had ever tasted.

After recruiting for a few days at the fort, and learning that there were large herds of the game, which they gloried most in hunting, the buffalo, near by, Carson and his party started for the stream on which they could be found, and were not long in discovering a large herd of fine fat buffalo. Stretching lines on which to hang the strips, they killed, and dressed, and cut; and soon had dried all the meat their animals could carry, when they returned to the fort.

Three days before reaching the fort, a party of Blackfeet Indians were again upon their trail, and watching for their return.

On the third morning after their arrival, just as day dawned, two of the Indians came past their camp to the *corral* of the fort in which their animals were confined, let down the bars and drove them all away; the sentinel, thinking the Indians were men of his party who had come to relieve his watch, had gone into camp and was soundly sleeping before the animals were missed. By this time the Indians had driven them many miles away, and as a similar *ruse* had been played upon the people at the fort a few days before, by which all their animals were run off, there was no possibility of giving chase.

Of course there was now no alternative but to wait the return of Captain McCoy from Walla Walla, which he did in about four weeks, bringing animals enough to supply Carson and his party, besides the men at the fort, which had been obtained of the Kiowas, or Kaious Indians, in Oregon. These Indians range between the Cascade and the Rocky Mountains, in what is now the eastern portion of Washington and Oregon Territories, living by the chase, and owning immense herds of horses, of which the chief of this tribe owned ten thousand. In this same locality the Indian bands, reported by the parties of trappers in the American Fur Company, had abundance of horses, with which they hunted deer, "ringing or surrounding them, and running them down in a circle." But while antelope, and elk, and deer, as well as beaver, were abundant, their locality was not frequented by the buffalo, its ranges being further toward the south and west.

Many suppose that buffalo never existed west of the Rocky Mountains; but to attempt a correction of this impression with our readers is no longer necessary, as we have seen Carson killing them on the Salmon River, on the Green River, and lastly, in the valley of a stream that flows into the Salmon.

From Baird's General Repository, published in 1857, we quote:

"It will perhaps excite surprise that I include the buffalo in the fauna of the Pacific States, as it is common to imagine that the buffalo has always been confined to the Atlantic slopes, because it does not now extend beyond the Rocky Mountains. This is not true. They once abounded on the Pacific."

This animal has not been found in California nor in Oregon, west of the Cascade Mountains, within the present generation of men, and the limit of its ranges, narrowing every year, is now far this side of the Rocky Mountains. Really a wild animal, incapable of being domesticated, as the country is more and more traversed, he retires—is killed by thousands by the hunter—and seems destined, as really as the Indian race, to become extinct. Could either be induced to adopt the modes of life which residence among the races of civilized men requires, their existence might be prolonged perhaps for centuries, but there seems to be no care, on the part of anybody who has the power, to preserve either the Indian or the buffalo as a distinct race of man, and quadruped.

A writer who reports his trip from California in the summer of '57, by Humboldt River and Fort Laramie, says:

"I watched for buffalo, expecting to see them in the valleys of the streams, the head-waters of the Platte. But the hundred miles upon the Sweet-water revealed no buffalo; upon the North Platte above Laramie there were none, and on the Fort Kearney we looked in vain for this noble game. If we had been a wagon party, and therefore confined to the road, this would not have surprised us, as the immense emigration to California first, to Salt Lake next, and the United States army following, might be supposed to have driven them away. Then, too, Colonel Sumner had been through, and with a war party of three hundred mounted riflemen, had followed the Cheyennes from Fort Laramie south to the head-waters of the Arkansas. But we frequently left the road for days together, in pursuit of game and the finer scenery of the immediate river valley, or the hills as it happened.

"Only until three days after passing Fort Kearney, did the glad sight greet us.

"In the broad bottom—ten miles at least between the hills that shut in the river valley—they were scattered thickly and quietly grazing.

"In two hours after coming in sight of them, we pitched our camp upon the river bank, and were soon prepared for the hunt. Though ten thousand were in sight, we had not yet approached within half a mile of one, so shy are they, moving off when we came in sight.

"The Platte was three-quarters of a mile wide where we were camped, and above and below us were numerous trails running from the river back into the hills. These were like the cow-paths running to a spring in a New England pasture. We camped about three o'clock, and soon after the buffalo upon one side of the stream commenced moving towards the river by these paths, and following each other close to wade across it in a continuous line by half a dozen paths in sight from where we were. These moving lines of huge animals were continued till slumber closed our eyes, at ten o'clock in the evening, and we knew not how much longer.

"Having no fresh animals, and only one that had not made the distance from the other side the Sierra Nevada within the last fifty days, we could not hunt by the chase. Accordingly, with nicely loaded double barreled rifle, we crept through the under-brush that lined the bank above us, and came near a line of buffalo crossing the river, and choosing our opportunity, as the animal pauses from the brisk trot before plunging into the stream, we were able to take good aim, and soon had lodged a ball in the breast of a fine cow, who with a bound leaped into the water, but was not able to proceed, nor needed the other shot which we lodged in the brain, to float her down the stream.

"Calling help, we had her dressed directly, and the nicest steaks upon the coals already kindled at the camp, and found them exceedingly delicious—of course more so from the fact that we had taken it. Others of the party came in without success; some had shot at a buffalo, others had got a sight of one, and at two of the crossings the line was broken temporarily by an unsuccessful attempt to kill an animal, but without hurting him. Most of us had no practise with this kind of game, though they had killed grouse, and some of them had shot antelope during our journey. But now their guns would not go off, or they shot too high, or could not get near enough. Just at dark, however, the old gentleman came in for help. His French rifle—a gun of Revolutionary times— had done execution, and a big bull was the prize he announced. We invited him to our prepared repast, but 'no! he would sup to-night upon his own game, he thanked us.' Of course he had the tongue from the animal he killed, nor were the tender-loin and other choice bits bad eating, and taking the tongue ourselves, with the rest of the party, (of ten,) we managed to carry away in the morning nearly all of the cow that we had not already eaten.

"All night long the bellowing from the other side the river greeted our tired senses. The situation was novel, and really in imagination, quite terrific. Would they return across the river and stampede our animals? We got a little sleep before midnight, but not much later.

"In the morning the buffalo were indeed returning in the style they went, but as we rode on over their track, the lines were always broken, and the animals scattered before we could approach them, and only once did we come within pistol shot of any of them; nor did the rest of the party do any better.

"Of course we might have done it had we made this our business; but we were hastening from the El Dorado after a four years' absence from our homes. So much for our *extemporized* buffalo hunting. In twenty-four hours after striking them, we had passed the buffalo, and saw no more of them. As we estimated it, we had seen in that time at least fifty thousand; we had crossed the trail of fifteen lines of them crossing the river after we left camp this morning."

We have quoted this to show the way in which travelers—emigrants now—meet the buffalo. Sometimes a huge drove of them overrun an emigrant party; but this seldom occurs, nor do parties often see more of them than did the one we have just presented, though usually they see them for a longer time. So much have the times changed since Carson was a trapper.

CHAPTER XIV.

WITH fresh animals, and men well fed and rested, McCoy and Carson and all their party soon started from Fort Hall, for the rendezvous again upon Green River, where they were detained some weeks for the arrival of other parties, enjoying as they best might the occasion and preparing for future operations.

A party of an hundred was here organized, with Mr. Fontenelle and Carson for its leaders, to trap upon the Yellowstone and the headwaters of the Missouri. It was known that they would probably meet the Blackfeet in whose grounds they were going, and it was therefore arranged, that, while fifty were to trap and furnish the food for the party, the remainder should be assigned to guard the camp and cook. There was no disinclination on the part of any to another meeting with the Blackfeet, so often had they troubled members of the party, especially Carson, who, while he could be **magnanimous** towards an enemy, would not turn aside from his course, if able to cope with him; and now he was in a company which justly felt itself strong enough to punish the " thieving Blackfeet," as they spoke of them, he was anxious to pay off some old scores.

They saw nothing, however, of these Indians; but afterwards learned that the smallpox had raged terribly among them, and that they had kept themselves retired in mountain valleys, oppressed with fear and severe disease.

The winter's encampment was made in this region, and a party of Crow Indians which was with them camped at a little distance, on the same stream. Here they had secured an abundance of meat, and passed the severe weather with a variety of amusements in which the Indians joined them in their lodges, made of buffalo hides. These lodges, very good substitutes for houses, are made in the form of a cone, spread by the means of poles spreading from a common center, where there was a hole at the top for the passage of the smoke. These were often twenty feet in height, and as many feet in diameter where they were pinned to the ground with stakes. In a large village the Indians often had one lodge large enough to hold fifty persons, and within were performed their war dances around a fire made in the center. During the palmy days of the British Fur Company, in a lodge like this, only made, instead of birch-bark, Irving says the Indians of the north held their " primitive fairs," outside the city of Montreal, where they disposed of their furs.

There was one drawback upon conviviality for this party, in the extreme difficulty of getting food for their animals ; for the food and fuel so abundant for themselves did not suffice for their horses. Snow covered the ground, and the trappers were obliged to gather willow twigs, and strip the bark from cottonwood trees, in order to keep them alive. The inner bark of the cottonwood is eaten by the Indians when reduced to extreme want. Besides, the cold brought the buffalo down upon them in large herds, to share the nourishment they had provided for their horses.

Spring at length opened, and gladly they again commenced trapping ; first on the Yellowstone, and soon on the head-waters of the Missouri, where they learned that the Blackfeet were recovered from the sickness of last year, which had not been so severe as it was reported, and that they were still anxious and in condition for a fight, and were encamped not far from their present trapping grounds.

Carson and five men went forward in advance " to reconnoiter," and found the village preparing to remove, having learned of the presence of the trappers. Hurrying back, a party of forty-three was selected from the whole, and they unanimously selected Carson to lead them, and leaving the rest to move on with the baggage, and aid them if it should be necessary when they should come up with the Indians, they hastened forward, eager for a battle.

Carson and his command were not long in overtaking the Indians, and dashing among them, at the first fire killed ten of their braves, but the Indians rallied, and retreated in good order. The white men were in fine spirits, and followed up their first attack with deadly result for three full hours, the Indians making scarce any resistance. Now their firing became less animated as their ammunition was getting low, and they had to use it with extreme caution. The Indians, suspecting this from the slackness of their fire, rallied, and with a tremendous whoop turned upon their enemies.

Now Carson and his company could use their small arms, which produced a terrible effect and which enabled them again to drive back the Indians. They rallied yet again, and charged with so much power, and in such numbers, they forced the trappers to retreat.

During this engagement, the horse of one of the mountaineers was killed, and fell with his whole weight upon his rider. Carson saw the condition of the man, with six warriors rushing to take his scalp, and reached the spot in time to save his friend. Leaping from the saddle, he placed himself before his fallen companion, shouting at the same time for his men to rally around him, and with deadly aim from his rifle shot down the foremost warrior.

The trappers now rallied about Carson, and the remaining five warriors retired, without the scalp of their fallen foe. Only two of them reached a place of safety; for the well aimed fire of the trappers leveled them with the earth.

Carson's horse was loose, and as his comrade was safe, he mounted behind one of his men, and rode back to the ranks, while, by general impulse, the firing upon both sides ceased. His horse was captured and restored to him, but each party, now thoroughly exhausted, seemed to wait for the other to renew the attack.

While resting in this attitude, the other division of the trappers came in sight, but the Indians, showing no fear, posted themselves among the rocks at some distance from the scene of the last skirmish, and coolly waited for their adversaries. Exhausted ammunition had been the cause of the retreat of Carson and his force, but now with a renewed supply, and an addition of fresh men to the force, they advanced on foot to drive the Indians from their hiding places. The contest was desperate and severe, but powder and ball eventually conquered, and the Indians, once dislodged, scattered in every direction. The trappers considered this a complete victory over the Blackfeet, for a large number of their warriors were killed, and many more were wounded, while they had but three men killed, and a few severely wounded.

Fontenelle and his party now camped at the scene of the engagement, to recruit their men and bury here their dead. Afterward they trapped through the whole Blackfeet country, and with great success; going where they pleased without fear or molestation. The Indians kept off their route, evidently having acquaintance with Carson and his company enough to last them their lifetime. With the smallpox and the white man's rifles the warriors were much reduced, and the tribe which had formerly numbered thirty thousand was already decimated, and a few more blows, like the one dealt by this dauntless band, would suffice to break its spirit, and destroy its power for future evil.

During the battle with the trappers, the women and children of the Blackfeet village were sent on in advance, and when the engagement was over, and the braves returned to them so much reduced in numbers, and without a single scalp, the big lodge that had been erected for the war dance was given up for the wounded, and in hundreds of Indian hearts grew a bitter hatred for the white man.

An express, despatched for the purpose, announced the place of the rendezvous to Fontenelle and Carson, who were now on Green River, and with their whole party and a large stock of furs, they at once set out for the place upon Mud River, to find the sales commenced before their arrival, so that in twenty days they were ready to break up camp.

Carson now organized a party of seven, and proceeded to a trading post called Brown's

Hole, where he joined a company of traders to go to the Navajoe Indians. He found this tribe more assimilated to the white man than any Indians he had yet seen, having many fine horses and large flocks of sheep and cattle. They also possessed the art of weaving, and their blankets were in great demand through Mexico, bringing high prices, on account of their great beauty, being woven in flowers with much taste. They were evidently a remnant of the Aztec race.

They traded here for a large drove of fine mules, which, taken to the fort on the South Platte, realized good prices, when Carson went again to Brown's Hole, a narrow but pretty valley about sixteen miles long, upon the Colorado River.

After many offers for his services from other parties, Carson at length engaged himself for the winter to hunt for the men at this fort, and as the game was abundant in this beautiful valley, and in the cañon country further down the Colorado, in its deer, elk, and antelope, reminding him of his hunts upon the Sacramento, the task was a delightful one to him.

In the Spring, Carson trapped with Bridger and Owens with passable success, and went to the rendezvous upon Wind River, at the head of the Yellowstone, and from thence, with a large part of the trappers at the rendezvous, to the Yellowstone, where they camped in the vicinity for the winter, without seeing their old enemy, the Blackfeet Indians, until midwinter, when they discovered that they were near their principal stronghold.

A party of forty was selected to give them battle, with Carson, of course, for their captain. They found the Indians already in the field, to the number of several hundred, who made a brave resistance, until night and darkness admonished both parties to retire. In the morning, when Carson and his men went to the spot whither the Indians had retired, they were not to be found. They had given them a "wide berth," taking their all away with them, even their dead.

Carson and his command returned to camp, where a council of war decided that as the Indians would report, at the principal encampment, the terrible loss they had sustained, and others would be sent to renew the fight, it was wise to prepare to act on the defensive, and use every precaution immediately; and accordingly a sentinel was stationed on a lofty hill near by.

who soon reported that the Indians were upon the move.

Their plans matured, they at once threw up a breastwork, under Carson's direction, and waited the approach of the Indians, who came in slowly, the first parties waiting for those behind. After three days, a full thousand had reached the camp, about half a mile from the breastwork of the trappers. In their war paint —stripes of red across the forehead, and down either cheek—with their bows and arrows, tomahawks, and lances, this army of Indians presented a formidable appearance to the small body of trappers who were opposed to them.

The war dance was enacted in sight and hearing of the trappers, and at early dawn the Indians advanced, having made every preparation for the attack. Carson commanded his men to reserve their fire till the Indians were near enough to have every shot tell; but seeing the strength of the white men's position, after a few ineffectual shots, the Indians retired, camped a mile from them, and finally separated into two parties, and went away, leaving the trappers to breathe more freely, for, at the best, the encounter must have been of a desperate character.

They evidently recognized the leader who had before dealt so severely with them, in the skill with which the defense was arranged, and if the name of Kit Carson was on their lips, they knew him for both bravery and magnanimity, and had not the courage to offer him battle.

Another winter gone, saddlery, moccasin-making, lodge-building, to complete the repairs of the summer's wars and the winter's fight, all completed, Carson with fifteen men went, past Fort Hall, again to the Salmon River, and trapped part of the season there and upon Big Snake and Goose Creeks, and selling his furs at Fort Hall, again joined Bridger in another trapping excursion into the Blackfeet country.

The Blackfeet had molested the traps of another party who had arrived there before them and had driven them away. The Indian assailants were still near, and Carson led his party against them, taking care to station himself and men in the edge of a thicket, where they kept the savages at bay all day, taking a man from their number with nearly every shot of their well directed rifles. In vain the Indians now attempted to fire the thicket; it would not burn, and suddenly they retired, forced again to acknowledge defeat at the hands of Kit Carson, the "Monarch of the prairies."

Carson's party now joined with the others, but concluding that they could not trap successfully with the annoyance the Indians were likely to give them, as their force was too small to hope to conquer, they left this part of the country for the north fork of the Missouri.

Now they were with the friendly Flatheads, one of whose chiefs joined them in the hunt, and went into camp near them, with a party of his braves. This tribe of Indians, like several other tribes which extend along this latitude to the Pacific, have the custom which gives them their name, thus described by Irving, in speaking of the Indians upon the Lower Columbia, about its mouth.

"A most singular custom," he says, "prevails, not only among the Chinooks, but among most of the tribes about this part of the coast, which is the flattening of the forehead. The process by which this deformity is effected, commences immediately after birth. The infant is laid in a wooden trough, by way of cradle. The end on which the head reposes is higher than the rest. A padding is placed on the forehead of the infant, with a piece of bark above it, and is pressed down by cords which pass through holes upon the sides of the trough. As the tightening of the padding and the pressure of the head to the board is gradual, the process is said not to be attended with pain. The appearance of the infant, however, while in this state of compression is whimsically hideous, and 'its little black eyes,' we are told, 'being forced out by the tightness of the bandages, resemble those of a mouse choked in a trap.'

"About a year's pressure is sufficient to produce the desired effect, at the end of which time, the child emerges from its bandages, a complete flathead, and continues so through life. It must be noted, however, that this flattening of the head has something in it of aristocratic significance, like the crippling of the feet among the Chinese ladies of quality. At any rate, it is the sign of freedom. No slave is permitted to bestow this deformity upon the head of his children; all the slaves, therefore, are roundheads."

CHAPTER XV.

In the spring, Kit Carson proposed a different plan of operations; he went to hunt on the streams in the vicinage of his winter's camp with only a single companion. The Utah Indians, into whose country he came, were also friends of Carson, and, unmolested in his business, his efforts were crowned with abundant success. He took his furs to Robideau Fort, and with a party of five went to Grand River, and thence to Brown's Hole on Green River for the winter.

In the following spring he went to the Utah country, to the streams that flow into Great Salt Lake on the South, which was rich in furs and of exceeding beauty, with the points of grand old snow mountains ever in sight, around him.

From here he went to the New Fork, and as it was afterward described by a party for whom Carson was the guide, we shall not give the description at this point of our narrative. Again he trapped among the Utahs, and disposed of his furs at Robideau Fort; but now the prices did not please him. Beaver fur was at a discount, and the trade of the trapper becoming unprofitable.

Baird, in his general report upon mammals, uses the following language, which is appropriate in this connection:

"The beaver once inhabited all of the globe lying in the northern temperate zone; yet from Europe, China, and all the eastern portion of the United States, it has been entirely exterminated, and a war so universal and relentless has been waged upon this defenseless animal, his great intelligence has been so generally opposed by the intelligence of man, it has seemed certain unless some kind providence should interpose that the castor, like its congener, the Castorides, would soon be found only in a fossil state.

"Happily that providence did interpose, through a certain ingenious somebody, who first suggested the use of silk in the place of fur for the covering of hats. The beaver were not yet exterminated from Western America, and now. since they are not "worth killing," in those in hospitable regions, where there is no encouragement for American enterprise or cupidity, we may hope that the beaver will there retain existence, in a home exclusively their own.

"The price of beaver skins had so much diminished that they were offered to some of the party at twenty-five cents by the bale.

Carson had pursued the business of trapping for eight years, and his life had been one of unceasing toil, of extreme hardship, full of danger, yet withal full of interest. More than this, while the lack of early scientific training had prevented him from making that record of his travels, which would have given the world the benefit of his explorations, he had treasured in his memory the knowledge of localities, of their conditions, and seasons, and advantages, which, in the good time coming, would enable him to associate his labors with another, who possessed the scientific attainments which Carson lacked, and who with Carson's invaluable assistance would come to be known world-wide as a bold explorer, and who, but for Carson's experience, where such experience was a chief requisite to success, might have failed in his first efforts in the grand enterprise entrusted to him.

Carson knew the general features of the country, its mountains, plains, and rivers, and the minor points of animal and vegetable pro ductions, from the head-waters of the " mon arch of rivers," to the mouth of the Colorado and from the southern Arkansas to the Columbia, better, perhaps, than any one living, though yet but twenty-five years of age.

We left Carson at Robideau Fort, tired of the pursuit of trapping, as soon as it had become unprofitable, and while there, he arranged with three or four other trappers to come down to Bent's Fort. The trip was like others made at this season, through a country where the rifle would supply food for the party, and arriving at Bent's Fort, where his name was already well known, Carson could not long be idle. He engaged himself to Messrs. Bent and St. Vrain, as hunter to the fort, preferring this by far to the idea of seeking employment nearer civilized life. Indeed no situation could have pleased him better, if we may judge from the fact that he continued in it for eight years, and until the connection with his employers was broken by the death of one of the partners, Colonel Bent.

Governor Bent, since appointed to the office of chief magistrate of New Mexico, by the United States Government, had been killed by Mexican Indians, and was universally mourned by Americans and Indians wherever he was known.

Mr. St. Vrain, the other partner, was active during the Mexican war, since the date of which we write, still lives, and is esteemed, as a father, by many an early mountaineer. Carson owed him gratitude for kindly sympathy and words of counsel, when yet a youth he was commencing his mountain life, and Dr. Peters, the first biographer of Kit Carson, dedicates his book to Colonel St. Vrain, asserting that he was the first to discover and direct Carson's talents to the path in which they were employed. For both of these gentlemanly proprietors, Carson cherished a warm friendship, nor was there ever an unpleasant occurrence between them.

When game was plenty, he supplied the forty mouths to be filled with ease, but when it was scarce, his task was sometimes difficult, but skill and experience enabled him to triumph over every obstacle.

It is not strange that with such long experience Carson became the most skilful of hunters, and won the name of the "Nestor of the Rocky Mountains." Among the Indians he had earned the undisputed title of "Monarch of the Prairies."

But while he killed thousands of elk, deer and antelope, nor disdained the rabbit and the grouse, and took the wild goose on the wing, of all the game of beast or bird, he liked the best to hunt the buffalo, for there was an excitement in the chase of that noble animal which aroused his spirits to the highest pitch of excitement.

Assuredly, Christopher Carson's *is* " a life out of the usual routine, and checkered with adventures which have sorely tested the courage and endurance of this wonderful man." Colonel St. Vrain, in the preface to Peters' Life of Carson, says:

" Entering upon his life work at the age of seventeen, choosing now to think for himself, nor follow the lead of those who would detain him in a quiet life, while he felt the restless fire ' in his bones,' that forbade his burying his energy in merely mechanical toil, he had yet been directed in his choice, by the fitness for it the pursuits of youth had given, and spurning the humdrum monotony of the shop, gave himself entirely to what would most aid him in attaining the profession he had chosen. We must admire such spirit in a youth, for it augurs well for the energy and will power of the manhood ; therefore, when the biographer says of Christopher Carson, that the neighbors who knew him predicted an uncommon life in the child with whom they hunted, and conceaed to him positions, as well as privileges, that were not accorded to common men, with his life till thirty-three before us, we feel that he has fulfilled the hope of early promise, with a noble manhood."

We have followed Carson's pathway, without much of detail, to the localities where he practised the profession he had chosen, until we saw him leave it because it ceased longer to afford compensation for his toil, and during as long a period we have written of his quiet pursuit of the, to him, pleasant, but laborious life of a hunter; unless we must class the latter eight years with the former, and assume each as a part of the profession he had chosen.

In all, with perhaps the exception of a few weeks at Santa Fé, when still in his minority, we have found him ever strong to resist the thousand temptations to evil with which his pathway was beset, and which drew other men away. Strong ever in the maintenance of the integrity of his manhood, even when the convivial circle and the game had a brief fascination for him, they taught him the lesson which he needed to learn, that only by earnest resistance, can evil be overcome; and thus he was enabled to admonish others against those temptations which had once overcome even his powers of resistance; and so he learned to school himself to the idea, that good comes ever through the temptation to evil to all those who have the courage to extract it.

We have followed him up and down all the streams of our great central western wilds, and indicated the store of geographic knowledge which he had acquired by hard experience before they were known so far to any one besides; and then for eight years more we have seen that this knowledge was digested and reviewed in the social circle with other mountain trappers, and beside the lonely mountain river, and 'neath the wild, steep cliff; or on the grassy bottom, or the barren plain, and in the less sterile places where the sage hen found a covert, and up among the oak openings, and in the gigantic parks, where, as a hunter, he revisited old haunts.

In all his toilsome and adventurous enterprises, while he sought to benefit himself, he never turned away, nor failed to lend a helping hand to a needy, suffering brother, or to encourage one who needed such a lesson, to turn his youth to the most account; and if affectionate regard is a recompense for such service, he had his compensation, as he passed along the path he had marked out for himself, not from the white man alone, but from the Indian who everywhere came to look upon Kit Carson as his friend.

The Comanches, the Arapahoes, the Utahs, and the Cheyennes, besides several smaller tribes, knew him personally in the hunt, and he had sat by their camp fires, and dandled their children, and sung to them the ditty,

"What makes the lamb love Mary so ?
The eager children cry ;
Why Mary loves the lamb, you know,
And that's the reason why."

The Indians feared, and reverenced, and loved him, and that this latter may be proved to the reader we relate the following story of private history, nor will it be esteemed out of taste:

The powerful Sioux had come from the north beyond their usual hunting grounds, and had had skirmishes with several Indian bands, some of whom sent for Carson to the Upper Arkansas to come over and help them drive back the

Sioux. As the larder at the fort was full, he consented to go with the war-painted Comanche messengers to a camp of their tribe, united with a band of Arapahoes. They told him the Sioux had a thousand warriors and many rifles, and they feared them, but knew that the "Monarch of the Prairies" could overcome them. Carson sat in council with the chiefs, and finally, instead of encouraging them to fight, persuaded them to peace, and acted so successfully the part of mediator, that the Sioux consented to retire from the hunting grounds of the Comanches when the season was over, and they separated without a collision.

It was while engaged as hunter for Messrs. Bent and St. Vrain, Carson took to himself an Indian wife, by whom he had a daughter still living, and who forms the connecting link between his past hardships and his present greatness; for that he is emphatically a great man, the whole civilized world has acknowledged.

The mother died soon after her birth, and Carson feeling that his rude cabin was scarcely the place to rear his child, determined, when of a suitable age, to take her to St. Louis, and secure for her those advantages of education which circumstances had denied to him: and accordingly, when his engagement at the fort had expired, he determined to go to St. Louis for that purpose, embracing on the route the opportunity of visiting the home of his boyhood, which he had not seen for sixteen years.

Of course he found everything changed. Many of those whom he had known as men and heads of families, were now grown old, while more had died off ; but by those to whom he was made known, he was recognized with a heartiness of welcome which brought tears to his eyes, though his heart was saddened at the changes which time had wrought. His fame had preceded him, and his welcome was therefore doubly cordial, for he had more than verified the promise of his youth.

Thence he proceeded to St. Louis, with the intention of placing his daughter at school, but here, to his great amazement, he found himself a lion ; for the advent of such a man in such a city, which had so often rung with his deeds of daring and suffering, could not be permitted to remain among its citizens unknown or unrecognized. He was courted and fêted, and, though gratified at the attentions showered upon him, found himself so thoroughly out of his element, that he longed to return to more pleasant and more familiar scenes, his old hunting grounds.

Having accomplished the object of his visit to St. Louis, in placing his daughter under proper guardianship, he left the city, carrying with him pleasing, because merited remembrances of the attentions paid to him, and leaving behind him impressions of the most favorable character.

Soon after he reached St. Louis, he had the good fortune to fall in with Lieutenant Fremont, who was there organizing a party for the exploration of the far western country, as yet unknown, and who was anxiously awaiting the arrival of Captain Drips, a well-known trader and trapper, who had been highly recommended to him as a guide.

Kit Carson's name and fame were familiar as household words to Fremont, and he gladly availed himself of his proffered services in lieu of those of Captain Drips. It did not take long for two such men as John C. Fremont and Kit Carson to become thoroughly acquainted with each other, and the accidental meeting at St. Louis resulted in the cementing of a friendship which has never been impaired,—won as it was on the one part by fidelity, truthfulness, integ rity, and courage, united to vast experience and consummate skill in the prosecution of the duty he had assumed—on the other by every quality which commands honor, regard, esteem, and high personal devotion.

And now Carson's life has commenced in earnest, for heretofore he has only been fitting himself to live. His name is embodied in the archives of our country's history, and no one has been more ready to accord to him the credit he so well earned, as has he who had the good fortune to secure, at the same time, the services of the most experienced guide of his day, and the devotion of a friend.

Lieutenant Fremont had instructions to explore and report upon the country lying between the frontiers of Missouri and the South Pass in the Rocky Mountains, on the line of the Kansas and Great Platte Rivers, and with his party, leaving St. Louis on the 22d of May, 1842, by steamboat for Chouteau's Landing on the Missouri, near the mouth of the Kansas, at a point twelve miles beyond at Chouteau's trading post, he encamped there to complete his arrangements for this important expedition.

CHAPTER XVI.

FREMONT was delayed several days at Chouteau's Landing, by the state of the weather, which prevented the necessary astronomical observations, but finally all his arrangements being completed, and the weather permitting, the party started in the highest spirit, and filled with anticipations of an exciting and adventurous journey.

He had collected in the neighborhood of St. Louis twenty-one men, principally Creole and Canadian *voyageurs*, who had become familiar with prairie life in the service of the fur companies in the Indian country. Mr. Charles Preuss, a native of Germany, was his assistant in the topographical part of the survey. L. Maxwell, of Kaskaskia, had been engaged as hunter, and Christopher Carson as guide.

Mr. Cyprian Chouteau, to whose kindness, during their stay at his house, all were much indebted, accompanied them several miles on their way, until they met an Indian, whom he had engaged to conduct them on the first thirty or forty miles, where he was to consign them to the ocean prairie, which stretched, without interruption, almost to the base of the Rocky Mountains.

During the journey, it was the customary practise to encamp an hour or two before sunset, when the carts were disposed so as to form a sort of barricade around a circle some eighty yards in diameter. The tents were pitched, and the horses hobbled and turned loose to graze; and but a few minutes elapsed before the cooks of the messes, of which there were four, were busily engaged in preparing the evening meal. At nightfall, the horses, mules, and oxen were driven in and picketed—that is, secured by a halter, of which one end was tied to a small steel-shod picket, and driven into the ground; the halter being twenty or thirty feet long, which enabled them to obtain a little food during the night. When they had reached a part of the country where such a precaution became necessary, the carts being regularly arranged for defending the camp, guard was mounted at eight o'clock, consisting of three men, who were relieved every two hours; the morning watch being horse guard for the day. At daybreak, the camp was roused, the animals turned loose to graze, and breakfast generally over between six and seven o'clock, when they resumed their march, making regularly a halt at noon for one or two hours. Such was usually the order of the day except when accident of country forced a variation, which, however, happened but rarely.

They reached the ford of the Kansas late in the afternoon of the 14th, where the river was two hundred and thirty yards wide, and commenced immediately preparations for crossing. The river had been swollen by the late rains, and was sweeping by with an angry current, yellow and turbid as the Missouri. Up to this point, the road traveled was a remarkably fine one, well beaten and level—the usual road of a prairie country. By this route, the ford was one hundred miles from the mouth of the Kansas River, on reaching which several mounted men led the way into the stream, to swim across. The animals were driven in after them, and in a few minutes all had reached the opposite bank in safety, with the exception of the oxen, which swam some distance down the river, and, returning to the right bank, were not got over until the next morning. In the meantime, the carts had been unloaded and dismantled, and an india-rubber boat, which had been brought for the survey of the Platte River, placed in the water. The boat was twenty feet long and five broad, and on it were placed the body and wheels of a cart, with the load belonging to it, and three men with paddles.

The velocity of the current, and the inconvenient freight, rendering it difficult to be managed, Basil Lajeunesse, one of the best swimmers, took in his teeth a line attached to the boat and swam ahead in order to reach a footing as soon as possible, and assist in drawing her over. In this manner, six passages had been successfully made, and as many carts with their contents, and a greater portion of the party, deposited on the left bank; but night was drawing near, and in his great anxiety to complete the crossing before darkness set in, he put on the boat, contrary to the advice of Carson, the last two carts with their loads. The consequence was, the boat was capsized, and everything on board was in a moment floating down stream. They were all, however, eventually recovered, but not without great trouble. Carson and Maxwell, who had been in the water nearly all the succeeding day, searching for the lost articles, were taken so ill in consequence of the prolonged exposure, the party was obliged to lie by another day to enable them to recruit, for to proceed without them would have been folly.

The dense timber which surrounded their camp, interfering with astronomical observations, and the wet and damaged stores requiring exposure to the sun, the tents were struck early the next day but one after this disaster, and the party moved up the river about seven miles, where they camped upon a handsome open prairie, some twenty feet above the water, and where the fine grass afforded a luxurious repast to the weary animals. They lay in camp here two days, during which time the men were kept busy in drying the provisions, painting the cart covers, and otherwise completing their equipage, until the afternoon when powder was distributed to them, and they spent some hours in firing at a mark, as they were now fairly in the Indian country, and it began to be time to prepare for the chances of the wilderness.

CHAPTER XVII.

Leaving the river bottom, the road which was the Oregon trail, past Fort Laramie, ran along the uplands, over a rolling country, upon which were scattered many boulders of red sandstone, some of them of several tons weight; and many beautiful plants and flowers enlivened the prairie. The barometer indicated fourteen hundred feet above the level of the sea, and the elevation appeared to have its influence on vegetation.

The country became more broken, rising still and covered everywhere with fragments of silicious limestone, strewn over the earth like pebbles on the seashore; especially upon the summits and exposed situations; and in these places but few plants grew, while in the creek bottoms, and ravines, a great variety of plants flourished.

For several days they continued their journey, annoyed only by the lack of water, and at length reached the range of the Pawnees who infested that part of the country, stealing horses from companies on their way to the mountains, and when in sufficient force, openly attacking them, and subjecting them to various insults; and it was while encamped here, that a regular guard was mounted for the first time, but the night passed over without annoyance.

Speaking of the constant watchfulness required when in the neighborhood of hostile or thieving Indians, Fremont says,

"The next morning we had a specimen of the false alarms to which all parties in these wild regions are subject. Proceeding up the valley, objects were seen on the opposite hills, which disappeared before a glass could be brought to bear upon them. A man, who was a short distance in the rear, came spurring up in great haste, shouting, Indians! Indians! He had been near enough to see and count them, according to his report, and had made out twenty-seven. I immediately halted; arms were examined and put in order; the usual preparations made; and Kit Carson, springing upon one of the hunting horses, crossed the river, and galloped off into the opposite prairies, to obtain some certain intelligence of their movements.

"Mounted on a fine horse, without a saddle, and scouring bareheaded over the prairies, Kit was one of the finest pictures of a horseman I have ever seen. A short time enabled him to discover that the Indian war party of twenty-seven consisted of six elk, who had been gazing curiously at our caravan as it passed by, and were now scampering off at full speed. This was our first alarm, and its excitement broke agreeably on the monotony of the day. At our noon halt, the men were exercised at a target; and in the evening we pitched our tents at a Pawnee encampment of last July. They had apparently killed buffalo here, as many bones were lying about, and the frames where the hides had been stretched were yet tanding."

Leaving the fork of the "Blue," upon a high dividing ridge, in about twenty-one miles they reached the coast of the Platte, or Nebraska River as it is called, a line of low hills, or the break from the prairie to the river bottom. Cacti here were numerous, and the *amorpha*, remarkable for its large and luxuriant purple clusters, was in full bloom. From the foot of the coast, two miles across the level bottom, brought them to the shore of the river twenty miles below the head of Grand Island, and more than three hundred from the mouth of the Kansas. The elevation of the Platte valley here was about two thousand feet above the level of the sea.

The next day they met a party of fourteen, who had started sixty days before from Fort Laramie, in barges laden with furs for the American Fur Company, hoping to come down the Platte without difficulty, as they left upon the annual flood, and their boats drew only nine inches of water. But at Scott's bluffs, one hundred and thirty miles below Fort Laramie, the river became so broad and shallow, and the current so changeful among the sand-bars, that they abandoned their boats and *cached* their cargoes, and were making the rest of their journey to St. Louis on foot, each with a pack as large as he could carry.

In the interchange of news, and the renewal of old acquaintanceships, they found wherewithal to fill a busy hour. Among them Fremont had found an old companion on the northern prairie, a hardened and hardly served veteran of the mountains, who had been as much hacked and scarred as an old *moustache* of Napoleon's " old guard." He flourished in the sobriquet of La Tulipe, and his real name no one knew. Finding that he was going to the States only because his company was bound in that direction, and that he was rather more willing to return with Fremont, he was taken again into his service.

A few days more of travel, whose monotony was not relieved by any incident worth narrating, brought the party in sight of the buffalo, swarming in immense numbers over the plains, where they had left scarcely a blade of grass standing. "Mr. Preuss," says Fremont, "who was sketching at a little distance in the rear, had at first noted them as large groves of timber. In the sight of such a mass of life, the traveler feels a strange emotion of grandeur. We had heard from a distance a dull and confused murmuring, and when we came in view of their dark masses, there was not one among us who did not feel his heart beat quicker. It was the early part of the day, when the herds are feeding; and everywhere they were in motion. Here and there a huge old bull was rolling in the grass, and clouds of dust rose in the air from various parts of the bands, each the scene of some obstinate fight. Indians and buffalo make the poetry and life of the prairie, and our camp was full of their exhilaration. In place of the quiet monotony of the march, relieved only by the cracking of the whip, and an '*avance donc! enfant de grace!*' shouts and songs resounded from every part of the line, and our evening camp was always the commencement of a feast, which terminated only with our departure on the following morning. At any time in the night might be seen pieces of the most delicate meat, roasting *en appolas*, on sticks around the fire, and the guard were never without company. With pleasant weather, and no enemy to fear, an abundance of the most excellent meat, and no scarcity of bread or tobacco, they were enjoying the oasis of a voyageur's life."

Three cows were killed on that day, but a serious accident befell Carson in the course of the chase, which had nearly cost him his life. Kit had shot one, and was continuing the chase in the midst of another herd, when his horse fell headlong, but sprang up and joined the flying band. Though considerably hurt, he had the good fortune to break no bones; and Maxwell, who was mounted on a fleet hunter, captured the runaway after a hard chase. He was on the point of shooting him, to avoid the loss of his bridle (a handsomely mounted Spanish one), when he found that his horse was able to come up with him.

This mishap, however, did not deter Kit from his favorite pursuit of buffalo-hunting, for on the following day, notwithstanding his really serious accident, we find him ready and eager for another chase. Fremont in his narrative thus relates the occurrence:—

"As we were riding quietly along the bank, a grand herd of buffalo, some seven or eight hundred in number, came crowding up from the river, where they had been to drink, and commenced crossing the plain slowly, eating as they went. The wind was favorable; the coolness of the morning invited to exercise; the ground was apparently good, and the distance across the prairie (two or three miles) gave us a fine opportunity to charge them before they could get among the river hills. It was too fine a prospect for a chase to be lost; and halting for a few moments, the hunters were brought up and saddled, and Kit Carson, Maxwell, and I, started together. They were now somewhat less than half a mile distant, and we rode easily along until within about three hundred yards, when a sudden agitation, a wavering in the band, and a galloping to and fro of some which were scattered along the skirts, gave us the intimation that we were discovered. We started together at a hand gallop, riding steadily abreast of each other, and here the interest of the chase became so engrossingly intense, that we were sensible to nothing else. We were now closing upon them rapidly, and the front of the mass was already in rapid motion for the hills, and in a few seconds the movement had communicated itself to the whole herd.

"A crowd of bulls, as usual, brought up the rear, and every now and then some of them faced about, and then dashed on after the band a short distance, and turned and looked again, as if more than half inclined to stand and fight. In a few moments, however, during which we had been quickening our pace, the rout was universal, and we were going over the ground like a hurricane. When at about thirty yards, we gave the usual shout (the hunter's *pas de charge*), and broke into the herd. We entered on the side, the mass giving way in every direction in their heedless course. Many of the bulls, less active and less fleet than the cows, paying no attention to the ground, and occupied solely with the hunter, were precipitated to the earth with great force, rolling over and over with the violence of the shock, and hardly distinguishable in the dust. We separated on entering, each singling out his game.

"My horse was a trained hunter, famous in the west under the name of Proveau, and with his eyes flashing, and the foam flying from his mouth, sprang on after the cow like a tiger. In a few moments he brought me alongside of her, and rising in the stirrups, I fired at the distance of a yard, the ball entering at the termination of the long hair, and passing near the heart. She fell headlong at the report of the gun, and, checking my horse, I looked around for my companions.

"At a little distance, Kit was on the ground, engaged in tying his horse to the horns of a cow which he was preparing to cut up. Among the scattered bands, at some distance below, I caught a glimpse of Maxwell; and while I was looking, a light wreath of white smoke curled away from his gun, from which I was too far to hear the report. Nearer, and between me and the hills, towards which they were directing their course, was the body of the herd, and giving my horse the rein, we dashed after them. A thick cloud of dust hung upon their rear, which filled my mouth and eyes, and nearly smothered me. In the midst of this I could see nothing, and the buffalo were not distinguishable until within thirty feet.

"They crowded together more densely still as I came upon them, and rushed along in such a compact body, that I could not obtain an entrance—the horse almost leaping upon them. In a few moments the mass divided to the right and left, the horns clattering with a noise heard above everything else, and my horse darted into the opening.

"Five or six bulls charged on us as we dashed along the line, but were left far behind; and singling out a cow, I gave her my fire, but struck too high. She gave a tremendous leap, and scoured on swifter than before. I reined up my horse, and the band swept on like a torrent, and left the place quiet and clear. Our chase had led us into dangerous ground. A prairie-dog village, so thickly settled that there were three or four holes in every twenty yards square, occupied the whole bottom for nearly two miles in length. Looking around, I saw only one of the hunters, nearly out of sight, and the long dark line of our caravan crawling along, three or four miles distant."

CHAPTER XVIII.

The encampment of the party on the 4th of July was a few miles from where the road crosses over to the north fork of the Platte, where a grand dinner was prepared, toasts drank, and salutes fired; and it was here Fremont decided to divide his party, wishing, himself, to explore the south fork of the Platte, as far as St. Vrain's Fort; and taking with him Maxwell and two others of his men, and the Cheyenne Indians, whose village was upon this river, he left the rest of the party to proceed under the direction of Clement Lambert up the north fork to Fort Laramie, where they were to wait his arrival, as he intended to cross the country between the two forts.

Buffalo were still plenty upon Fremont's route, and the Indians with him made an unsuccessful attempt to lasso the leader of a drove of wild horses, which they passed. They met a band of two or three hundred Arapahoe Indians, and were only saved from an attack by Maxwell, who secured a timely recognition from the old chief who led the party, which proved to be from a village among whom he had resided as a trader, and whose camp the chief pointed out to them some six miles distant. They had come out to surround a band of buffalo which was feeding across the river, and were making a large circuit to avoid giving them the wind, when they discovered Fremont's party, whom they had mistaken for Pawnees. In a few minutes the women came galloping up, astride of their horses, and naked from their knees down, and the hips up. They followed the men to assist in cutting up and carrying off the meat.

The wind was blowing directly across the river, and the chief having requested Fremont to remain where he then was, to avoid raising the herd, he readily consented, and having unsaddled their horses, they sat down to view the scene. The day had become very hot, the thermometer standing at 108°. The Indians commenced crossing the river, and as soon as they were upon the other side, separated into two bodies.

Fremont thus describes this exciting hunt, or massacre, as the reader may choose to des ignate it, and his subsequent visit to the Arapahoe village:

"One party proceeded directly across the prairie, towards the hills, in an extended line, while the other went up the river; and instantly, as they had given the wind to the herd, the chase commenced. The buffalo started for the hills, but were intercepted and driven back toward the river, broken and running in every direction. The clouds of dust soon covered the whole scene, preventing us from having any but an occasional view. It had a very singular appearance to us at a distance, especially when looking with the glass.

"We were too far to hear the report of the guns, or any sound, and at every instant, through the clouds of dust, which the sun made luminous, we could see for a moment two or three buffalo dashing along, and close behind them an Indian with his long spear, or other weapon, and instantly again they disappeared. The apparent silence, and the dimly seen figures flitting by with such rapidity, gave it a kind of dreamy effect, and seemed more like a picture than a scene of real life.

"It had been a large herd when the *cerne* commenced, probably three or four hundred in number; but though I watched them closely, I did not see one emerge from the fatal cloud where the work of destruction was going on. After remaining here about an hour, we resumed our journey in the direction of the village.

"Gradually, as we rode on, Indian after Indian came dropping along, laden with meat; and by the time we had reached the lodges, the backward road was covered with the returning horsemen. It was a pleasant contrast with the desert road we had been traveling. Several had joined company with us, and one of the chiefs invited us to his lodge.

"The village consisted of about one hundred and twenty-five lodges, of which twenty were Cheyennes; the latter pitched a little apart from the Arapahoes. They were disposed in a scattering manner on both sides of a broad, irregular street, about one hundred and fifty feet wide, and running along the river. As we rode along, I remarked near some of the lodges a kind of tripod frame, formed of three slender poles of birch, scraped very clean, to which were affixed the shield and spear, with some other weapons of a chief. All were scrupulously clean, the spear head was burnished bright, and the shield white and stainless. It reminded me of the days of feudal chivalry ; and when, as I rode by, I yielded to the passing impulse, and touched one of the spotless shields with the muzzle of my gun, I almost expected a grim warrior to start from the lodge and resent my challenge.

"The master of the lodge spread out a robe for me to sit upon, and the squaws set before us a large wooden dish of buffalo meat. He had lit his pipe in the meanwhile, and when it had been passed around, we commenced our dinner while he continued to smoke. Gradually, five or six other chiefs came in, and took their seats in silence. When we had finished our host asked a number of questions relative to the object of our journey, of which I made no concealment; telling him simply that I had made a visit to see the country, preparatory to the establishment of military posts on the way to the mountains.

"Although this was information of the highest interest to them, and by no means calculated to please them, it excited no expression of surprise, and in no way altered the grave courtesy of their demeanor. The others listened and smoked. I remarked, that in taking the pipe for the first time, each had turned the stem upward, with a rapid glance, as in offering to the Great Spirit, before he put it in his mouth."

Riding near the river, Fremont and Maxwell had an interview with Jim Beckwith, who had been chief of the Crow Indians, but had left them some time before, and was now residing in this river bottom, with his wife, a Spanish woman from Taos. They also passed a camp of four or five New Englanders, with Indian wives—a party of independent trappers, and reached St. Vrain's Fort on the evening of July 10th, where they were hospitably entertained by Mr. St. Vrain, and received from him such needed assistance as he was able to render. Maxwell was at home here, as he had spent the last two or three years between the fort and Taos.

On the evening of the fifteenth, they arrived at Fort Laramie, a post of the American Fur Company, near the junction of the Laramie Creek with the Platte River, which had quite a military appearance, with its lofty walls whitewashed and picketed, and large bastions at the angles. A cluster of lodges belonging to the Sioux Indians was pitched under the walls. He was received with great hospitality by the gentleman in charge of the fort, Mr. Boudeau

having letters of introduction to him from the
company at St. Louis, and it is hardly necessary
to say that he was hospitably received and most
kindly treated. He found Carson with the
party under his command camped on the bank
near the fort, by whom they were most warmly
welcomed, and in the enjoyment of a bountiful
supper, which coffee and bread converted almost
into a luxury, they forgot the toils and sufferings of the past ten days.

The news brought by Mr. Preuss, who it will
be remembered was with Carson's party, was
as exciting as it was unpleasant. He had learned
that the Sioux, who had been badly disposed,
had now broken out into open hostilities, and
his informant, a well-known trapper, named
Bridger, had been attacked by them, and had
only defeated them after serious losses on both
sides. United with the Cheyennes and Gros
Ventre Indians, they were scouring the country
in war parties, declaring war upon every living
thing which should pass the *Red Buttes;* their
special hostility being, however, directed
against the white men. In fact the country
was swarming with hostile Indians, and it was
but too evident that any party who should attempt to enter upon the forbidden grounds, must

do so at the certain hazard of their lives. Of course such intelligence created great emotion throughout the camp, and it formed the sole subject of conversation and discussion during the evenings around the camp fires.

Speaking of this report, and the effect produced upon his men, Fremont uses the following language:

"Carson, one of the best and most experienced mountaineers, fully supported the opinion given by Bridger of the dangerous state of the country, and openly expressed his conviction that we could not escape without some sharp encounters with the Indians. In addition to this, he made his will; and among the circumstances which were constantly occurring to increase their alarm, this was the most unfortunate; and I found that a number of my party had become so much intimidated that they had requested to be discharged at this place."

Carson's apprehensions were fully justified by the circumstances surrounding them; and while we might have omitted the above quotation, as tending to exhibit him in a false light, doubtless unintentionally, we choose rather to say a few words which will rob the insinuation of its sting.

While there was reason to expect an encounter with Indians, in whom it was reported the spirit of revenge was cherished towards the whites, more than ever it had been before, and whom numbers and acquisition of firearms rendered really formidable foes, he felt that the party with whom he was now associated, were not the men upon whom he could rely with certainty in an engagement against such terrible odds. In the days of his earlier experiences, the old trappers with him were men who had as little fear as himself, and were also experienced in such little affairs, for such they considered them. Now, except Maxwell, an old associate, and two or three others, the men of the party were half paralyzed with fear at the prospect which this report presented to them; and it was the knowledge of their fear, which they made no attempt to conceal, which excited in his mind apprehensions for the worst, for he did not choose to guide others into danger recklessly, even if he had no care for himself.

Headlong rashness, which some might mistake for courage, was not a trait of his character; but the voice of a whole country accords to him cool bravery, presence of mind, and courage to meet whatever danger forethought could not guard against.

With a party of men like those he had led several times against the Blackfeet, nothing could have persuaded him to turn back from any enterprise which he had undertaken, from a fear of hostile Indians. Of course he could not state his reason for his apprehensions even to his employer, because it would reflect upon his ability to arrange for such an enterprise, or his courage to conduct it to a successful termination, neither of which he could doubt; and it is therefore with something of regret we read in an official report, emanating from one who owed more to Kit Carson, of the fame and reputation so justly earned, than to any other living man, the assertion that Carson, stimulated by fear, made his will. The best contradiction which can be afforded is found in the fact that, notwithstanding his *apprehensions*, he did accompany the party, discharging with his usual zeal, ability, and fidelity, the duties which devolved upon him; and we have yet to learn that Kit Carson ever shrunk from any danger.

His reputation has, however, outlived this covert insinuation, and we presume that no man on this continent would hesitate to award to

Kit Carson the highest attributes of moral and physical courage.

"During our stay here," says Fremont in continuation, "the men had been engaged in making numerous repairs, arranging pack-saddles, and otherwise preparing for the chances of a rough road and mountain travel, all of which Carson had superintended, urging upon the men that their comfort and their safety required it. All things of this nature being ready, I gathered them around me in the evening, and told them that I had determined to proceed the next day. They were all well armed. I had engaged the services of Mr. Bissonette as interpreter, and had taken, in the circumstances, every possible means to insure our safety. In the rumors we had heard, I believed there was much exaggeration, and then they were men accustomed to this kind of life, and to the country; and that these were the dangers of everyday occurrence, and to be expected in the ordinary course of their service. They had heard of the unsettled condition of the country before leaving St. Louis, and therefore could not make it a reason for breaking their engagements. Still I was unwilling to take with me, on a service of some certain danger. men on whom I could not rely; and as I had understood that there were among them some who were disposed to cowardice, and anxious to return, they had but to come forward at once, and state their desire, and they would be discharged with the amount due to them for the time they had served." To their honor, be it said, there was but one among them who had the face to come forward and avail himself of the permission. I asked him some few questions, in order to expose him to the ridicule of the men, and let him go. The day after our departure, he engaged himself to one of the forts, and set off with a party to the Upper Missouri.

CHAPTER XIX.

As our explorers advanced, one of the most prominent features of the country was the abundance of artemisia growing everywhere, on the hills and in the river bottoms, in twisted wiry clumps, filling the air with the odor of mingled camphor and spirits of turpentine, and impeding the progress of the wagons out of the beaten track.

They met a straggling party of the Indians which had followed the trail of the emigrants, and learned from them that multitudes of grasshoppers had consumed the grass upon the road, so that they had found no game, and were obliged to kill even their horses, to ward off starvation. Of course danger from these Indians was no longer to be apprehended, though the prospect was a gloomy one, but new courage seemed to inspire the party when the necessity of endurance seemed at hand.

The party now followed Carson's advice given at Fort Laramie, to disencumber them selves of all unnecessary articles, and accordingly they left their wagons, concealing them among low shrubbery, after they had taken them to pieces, and made a *cache* of such other effects as they could leave, among the sand heaps of the river bank, and then set to work to mend and arrange the pack-saddles and packs, the whole of which was superintended by Carson, and to him was now assigned the office of guide, as they had reached a section of the country, with a great part of which long residence had made him familiar. Game was found in great abundance after they reached the river bottom, off the traveled road, both upon the Platte and after they crossed over the *divide* to the Sweet Water.

Speaking of the gorge where the Platte River issues from the Black Hills, changing its character abruptly from a mountain stream to a river of the plain, Fremont says, "I visited this place with *my favorite man*, Basil Lajeunesse;" and this extraordinary expression, left unexplained, would lead the casual reader to believe or think that Carson had lost the confidence of the *official* leader of the party.

It has seemed to us, in reading Fremont's narrative of this first expedition to the Rocky

Mountains, that in view of some failures to achieve what was sought, and to avoid what was suffered, Carson's advice, given with a larger experience, and with less of impetuosity, than that of the young Huguenot's, would, if followed, have secured different results, both for the comfort of the party, and the benefit of science; and while those of like temperament were chosen for companions by Lieutenant Fremont, it detracts nothing from his reputation for scientific analysis and skill, or for high courage, but only gives to Carson the deserved meed of praise to say, his was the hand that steadied the helm, and kept the vessel on her way, at times when, without his judgment, sagacity, and experience, it must have been seriously damaged, if not destroyed; and with this balance wheel, a part of his machinery, the variety of difficulties that might have defeated the scientific purpose of the expedition, or have made it the last Fremont would desire, or the Government care to have him undertake, were avoided; and no one inquired to know the cause.

It often happens that the quiet, simpler offices of life become imperative, and first duties, to one who feels that all the qualifications fitting for more honorable place, are possessed by him, in much larger measure than by the occupant of the higher official position,—as men are wont to esteem it—and, as there is no explanation given, nor, by declaration, even the fact stated that this was true now in respect to Christopher Carson, we shall give no reason, further than to say, that the care of finding suitable places for camping, of seeing that the party were all in, and the animals properly cared for, their saddles in order, and the fastenings secure; of finding game, and watching to see that the food is properly expended, so that each supply shall last till it can be replenished; of seeing that the general property of the party is properly guarded, and a variety of other matters, which pertain to the success of an enterprise like this, and without which it must be a failure, could not all be borne by Fremont; and while he had assigned to each his position in the labor of the camp, the place of general care-taker, which comes not by appointment, fell naturally to the lot of Carson; and such supervision was cheerfully performed though it brought no other reward than the satisfaction of knowing that the essential elements of success were not neglected.

Shall we not then deem him worthy of all

praise for being content to occupy such a position? Employed to guide the party, he had hoped to share the confidence of its leader, but the latter had already other friends, jealous of his attentions; he had another hunter, jealous of his own reputation in his profession, and of his knowledge of the country; then there were two youths in the party, one of whom wished to be amused and both to be instructed; and in becoming the general providence of the party, which is scarcely thought of, because it seems to come of itself, we find the reason why Fremont's first narrative shows Carson so little like the brave, bold hunter we have known him hitherto. We allude to two lads, one a son of the Hon. T. H. Benton, who accompanied him out during a portion of his first expedition, and for whom it is evident he made many sacrifices.

Buffalo were numerous, and they saw many tracks of the grizzly bear among the cherry trees and currant bushes that lined the river banks, while antelope bounded fitfully before them over the plains.

But the reader is already familiar with this condition of things in the country, because the hero of our story has been here before, and to apply the term explorer here to Fremont, and to call this an exploring expedition, seems farcical, only as we remember that there had not been yet any written scientific description of this region, so long familiar to the trappers and to none more than Carson.

They had now approached the road at what is called the South Pass. The ascent had been so gradual, that, with all the intimate knowledge possessed by Carson, who had made this country his home for seventeen years, they were obliged to watch very closely to find the place at which they reached the culminating point. This was between two low hills, rising on either hand fifty or sixty feet.

Approaching it from the mouth of the Sweet Water, a sandy plain, one hundred and twenty miles long, conducts, by a gradual and regular ascent, to the summit, about seven thousand feet above the sea; and the traveler, without being reminded of any change by toilsome ascents, suddenly finds himself on the waters which flow to the Pacific Ocean. By the route they had traveled, the distance from Fort Laramie was three hundred and twenty miles, or nine hundred and fifty from the mouth of the Kansas.

They continued on till they came to a tributary of the Green River, and then followed the stream up to a lake at its source in the mountains, and had here a view of extraordinary magnificence and grandeur, beyond what is seen in any part of the Alps, and here, beside the placid lake, they left the mules, intending to ascend the mountains on foot, and measure the altitude of the highest point.

Fremont had wished to make a circuit of a few miles in the mountains, and visit the sources of the four great streams, the Colorado, the Columbia, the Missouri, and the Platte, but game was scarce, and his men were not accustomed to their entirely meat fare, and were discontented.

With fifteen picked men, mounted on the best mules, was commenced the ascent of the mountains, and amid views of most romantic beauty, overlooking deep valleys with lakes nestled in them, surrounded by precipitous ridges, hundreds of feet high, they wound their way up to the summits of the ridges, to descend again, and plod along the valley of a little stream on the other side.

For two days they continued upon their mules, through this magnificent region, when the peak appeared so near, it was decided to leave the mules beside a little lake, and proceed on foot; and as the day was warm, some of the party left their coats. But at night they had reached the limit of the piney region, when they were ten thousand feet above the waters of the Gulf of Mexico, and still the peak rose far above them, so that they camped without suffering, in a little green ravine, bordered with plants in bloom, and the next morning continued the ascent. Carson had led this day, and succeeded in reaching the summit of a snowy peak, supposed to be the highest, but saw from it the one they had been seeking, towering eight hundred or a thousand feet above him. They now descended off the snow and sent back for mules, and food, and blankets, and by a blazing fire all slept soundly until morning.

Carson had understood that they had now done with the mountains, and by directions had gone at daybreak to the camp, taking with him all but four or five men, who were to remain with Fremont, and take back the mules and instruments. But after their departure, the program was changed, and now understanding the topography of the country better, the party left, continued with the mules as far as possible, and then on foot over chasms, leaping irom point to point of crags, until they came, with extreme difficulty, in the intense cold and rarefied air, to the height of the crest, and Fremont stood alone upon the pinnacle, and able to tell the story of this victory of Science to the world. He had been sick the day before, and Carson could not urge the prosecution of the enterprise, to reach the highest point, when the leader of the expedition was too ill to climb the summit, and therefore had not objected to the arrangement of returning to the camp.

But we have nothing more to say. The reader of the story, as Fremont tells it, wishes there were evidences of higher magnanimity, which are wanting. Carson finds no fault, seems to notice none. He performed faithfully the duty assigned to him, utters no complaint, but is content in carrying out a subordinate's first obligation, that of obeying orders.

CHAPTER XX.

FREMONT succeeded, but not without much danger and suffering, in reaching the highest peak of the Rocky Mountains, and waved over it his country's flag, in triumph. The return trip to Fort Laramie was not marked by any incident of special note, and Carson's services being no longer required, he left his commander here, and set out for New Mexico. In 1843, he married a Spanish lady, and his time was occasionally employed by Messrs. Bent and St. Vrain, his old and tried friends.

While thus engaged at Bent's Fort he learned that his old commander and friend had passed two days before, on another exploring expedition, and being naturally anxious to see again one to whom he was so strongly attached, he started on his trail, and after following it for seventy miles, came up with him. The meeting was mutually pleasing, but resulted quite contrary to Carson's anticipations, for, instead of merely meeting and parting, Fremont, anxious to regain the services of one whose experience, judgment, and courage had been so well tried, persuaded him to join this second expedition and again we find him launched as guide and hunter.

Carson was at once despatched to the fort with directions to procure a supply of mules, which the party much needed, and to meet him with the animals at St. Vrain's Fort. This was accomplished to Fremont's entire satisfaction. The object of this second exploration was to connect the survey of the previous year with those of Commander Wilkes on the Pacific coast, but Fremont's first destination was the Great Salt Lake, which has since become so famous in the annals of our country.

Fremont's description of this journey, and of his passage across the lake in a frail india-rubber boat, which threatened at every moment destruction to the entire party, is so true to life, and so highly interesting, we quote it entire. The party reached, on the 21st of August, the Bear River, which was the principal tributary of the lake, and from this point we quote Fremont's words:

"We were now entering a region which, for us, possessed a strange and extraordinary interest. We were upon the waters of the famous lake which forms a salient point among the remarkable geographical features of the country, and around which the vague and superstitious accounts of the trappers had thrown a delightful obscurity, which we anticipated pleasure in dispelling, but which, in the meantime, left a crowded field for the exercise of our imagination.

"In our occasional conversations with the few old hunters who had visited the region, it had been a subject of frequent speculation; and the wonders which they related were not the less agreeable because they were highly exaggerated and impossible.

"Hitherto this lake had been seen only by trappers, who were wandering through the country in search of new beaver streams, caring very little for geography; its islands had never been visited; and none were to be found who had entirely made the circuit of its shores and no instrumental observations, or geographical survey of any description, had ever been made anywhere in the neighboring region. It was generally supposed that it had no visible outlet; but, among the trappers, including those in my own camp, were many who believed that somewhere on its surface was a terrible whirlpool, through which its waters found their way to the ocean by some subterranean communication. All these things had been made a frequent subject of discussion in our desultory conversations around the fires at night; and my own mind had become tolerably well filled with their indefinite pictures, and insensibly colored with their romantic descriptions, which, in the pleasure of excitement, I was well disposed to believe, and half expected to realize.

" In about six miles' travel from our encampment, we reached one of the points in our journey to which we had always looked forward with great interest—the famous Beer Springs, which, on account of the effervescing gas and acid taste, had received their name from the voyageurs and trappers of the country, who, in the midst of their rude and hard lives, are fond of finding some fancied resemblance to the luxuries they rarely have the good fortune to enjoy.

" Although somewhat disappointed in the expectations which various descriptions had led me to form of unusual beauty of situation and scenery, I found it altogether a place of very great interest; and a traveler for the first time in a volcanic region remains in a constant excitement, and at every step is arrested by something remarkable and new. There is a confusion of interesting objects gathered together in a small space. Around the place of encampment the Beer Springs were numerous; but, as far as we could ascertain, were entirely confined to that locality in the bottom. In the bed of the river, in front, for a space of several hundred yards, they were very abundant; the effervescing gas rising up and agitating the water in countless bubbling columns. In the vicinity round about were numerous springs of an entirely different and equally marked mineral character. In a rather picturesque spot, about 1,300 yards below our encampment and immediately on the river bank, is the most remarkable spring of the place. In an opening on the rock, a white column of scattered water is thrown up, in form like a *jet-d'eau*, to a variable height of about three feet, and, though it is maintained in a constant supply, its greatest height is attained only at regular intervals, according to the action of the force below. It is accompanied by a subterranean noise, which, together with the motion of the water, makes very much the impression of a steamboat in motion; and, without knowing that it had been already previously so called, we gave to it the name of the Steamboat Spring. The rock through which it is forced is slightly raised in a convex manner, and gathered at the opening into an urn-mouthed form, and is evidently formed by continued deposition from the water, and colored bright red by oxide of iron.

"It is a hot spring, and the water has a pungent, disagreeable metallic taste, leaving a burning effect on the tongue. Within perhaps two yards of the *jet-d'eau*, is a small hole of about an inch in diameter, through which, at regular intervals, escapes a blast of hot air with a light wreath of smoke, accompanied by a regular noise.

"As they approached the lake, they passed over a country of bold and striking scenery and through several 'gates,' as they called certain narrow valleys. The 'standing rock' is a huge column, occupying the center of one of these passes. It fell from a height of perhaps 3,000 feet, and happened to remain in its present upright position.

"At last, on the 6th of September, the object for which their eyes had long been straining was brought to view.

"*Sept.* 6.—This time we reached the butte

without any difficulty; and, ascending to the summit, immediately at our feet beheld the object of our anxious search, the waters of the Inland Sea, stretching in still and solitary grandeur far beyond the limit of our vision. It was one of the great points of the exploration; and as we looked eagerly over the lake in the first emotions of excited pleasure I am doubtful if the followers of Balboa felt more enthusiasm when, from the heights of the Andes, they saw for the first time the great Western Ocean. It was certainly a magnificent object, and a noble *terminus* to this part of our expedition; and to travelers so long shut up among amountain ranges, a sudden view over the expanse of silent waters had in it something sublime. Several large islands raised their high rocky heads out of the waves; but whether or not they were timbered was still left to our imagination, as the distance was too great to determine if the dark hues upon them were woodland or naked rock. During the day the clouds had been gathering black over the mountains to the westward, and while we were looking, a storm burst down with sudden fury upon the lake, and entirely hid the islands from our view.

"On the edge of the stream a favorable spot was selected in a grove, and, felling the timber, we made a strong *corral*, or horse-pen, for the animals, and a little fort for the people who were to remain. We were now probably in the country of the Utah Indians, though none reside upon the lake. The india-rubber boat was repaired with prepared cloth and gum, and filled with air, in readiness for the next day.

"The provisions which Carson had brought with him being now exhausted, and our stock reduced to a small quantity of roots, I determined to retain with me only a sufficient number of men for the execution of our design; and accordingly seven were sent back to Fort Hall, under the guidance of François Lajeunesse, who, having been for many years a trapper in the country, was an experienced mountaineer.

"We formed now but a small family. With Mr. Preuss and myself, Carson, Bernier, and Basil Lajeunesse had been selected for the boat expedition—the first ever attempted on this interior sea; and Badau, with Derosier, and Jacob (the colored man), were to be left in charge of the camp. We were favored with most delightful weather To-night there was a brilliant sunset of golden orange and green, which left the western sky clear and beautifully pure; but clouds in the east made me lose an occultation. The summer frogs were singing around us, and the evening was very pleasant, with a temperature of 60°—a night of a more southern autumn. For our supper, we had *yampah*, the most agreeably flavored of the roots, seasoned by a small fat duck, which had come in the way of Jacob's rifle. Around our fire to-night were many speculations on what to-morrow would bring forth; and in our busy conjectures we fancied that we should find every one of the large islands a tangled wilderness of trees and shrubbery, teeming with game of every description that the neighboring region afforded, and which the foot of a white man or Indian had never violated. Frequently, during the day, clouds had rested on the summits of their lofty mountains, and we believed that we should find clear streams and springs of fresh water; and we indulged in anticipations of the luxurious repasts with which we were to indemnify ourselves for past privations. Neither, in our discussions, were the whirlpool and other mysterious dangers forgotten, which Indian and hunters' stories attributed to this unexplored lake. The men had discovered that, instead of being strongly sewed (like that of the preceding year, which had so triumphantly rode the cañons of the Upper Great Platte), our present boat was only pasted together in a very insecure manner, the maker having been allowed so little time in the construction that he was obliged to crowd the labor of two months into several days. The insecurity of the boat was sensibly felt by us; and mingled with the enthusiasm and excitement that we all felt at the prospect of an undertaking which had never before been accomplished, was a certain impression of danger, sufficient to give a serious character to our conversation. The momentary view which had been had of the lake the day before, its great extent, and rugged islands, dimly seen amidst the dark waters in the obscurity of the sudden storm, were well calculated to heighten the idea of undefined danger with which the lake was generally associated.

"*Sept.* 8.—A calm, clear day, with a sunrise temperature of 41°. In view of our present enterprise, a part of the equipment of the boat had been made to consist of three airtight bags, about three feet long, and capable each of containing five gallons. These had been tilled with water the night before, and were now placed in the boat, with our blankets and instruments, consisting of a sextant, telescope, spy-glass, thermometer, and barometer.

"In the course of the morning we discovered that two of the cylinders leaked so much as to require one man constantly at the bellows, to keep them sufficiently full of air to support the boat. Although we had made a very early start, we loitered so much on the way—stopping every now and then, and floating silently along, to get a shot at a goose or a duck—that it was late in the day when we reached the outlet. The river here divided into several branches, filled with fluvials, and so very shallow that it was with difficulty we could get the boat along, being obliged to get out and wade. We encamped on a low point among rushes and young willows, where there was a quantity of driftwood, which served for our fires. The evening was mild and clear; we made a pleasant bed of the young willows; and geese and ducks enough had been killed for an abundant supper at night, and for breakfast next morning. The stillness of the night was enlivened by millions of water-fowl.

"*Sept.* 9.—The day was clear and calm;

the thermometer at sunrise at 49°. As is usual with the trappers on the eve of any enterprise, our people had made dreams, and theirs happened to be a bad one—one which always preceded evil—and consequently they looked very gloomy this morning ; but we hurried through our breakfast, in order to make an early start, and have all the day before us for our adventure. The channel in a short distance became so shallow that our navigation was at an end, being merely a sheet of soft mud, with a few inches of water, and sometimes none at all, forming the low-water shore of the lake. All this place was absolutely covered with flocks of screaming plover. We took off our clothes, and, getting overboard, commenced dragging the boat—making, by this operation, a very curious trail, and a very disagreeable smell in stirring up the mud, as we sank above the knee at every step. The water here was still fresh, with only an insipid and disagreeable taste, probably derived from the bed of fetid mud. After proceeding in this way about a mile, we came to a small black ridge on the bottom, beyond which the water became suddenly salt, beginning gradually to deepen, and the bottom was sandy and firm. It was a re markable division, separating the fresh water of the rivers from the briny water of the lake, which was entirely *saturated* with common salt. Pushing our little vessel across the narrow boundary, we sprang on board, and at length were afloat on the waters of the unknown sea.

"We did not steer for the mountainous islands, but directed our course towards a lower one, which it had been decided we should first visit, the summit of which was formed like the crater at the upper end of Bear River valley. So long as we could touch the bottom with our paddles, we were very gay; but gradually, as the water deepened, we became more still in our frail batteau of gum cloth distended with air, and with pasted seams. Although the day was very calm, there was a considerable swell on the lake; and there were white patches of foam on the surface, which were slowly moving to the southward, indicating the set of a current in that direction, and recalling the recollection of the whirlpool stories. The water continued to deepen as we advanced; the lake becoming almost transparently clear, of an extremely beautiful bright green color; and the spray, which was thrown into the boat and over our clothes, was directly converted into a crust of common salt, which covered also our hands and arms. 'Captain,' said Carson, who for some time had been looking suspiciously at some whitening appearances outside the nearest islands, 'what are those yonder?—won't you just take a look with the glass?' We ceased paddling for a moment, and found them to be the caps of the waves that were beginning to break under the force of a strong breeze that was coming up the lake. The form of the boat seemed to be an admirable one, and it rode on the waves like a water bird; but at the same time, it was extremely slow in its progress. When we were a little more than half way across the reach, two of the divisions between the cylinders gave way, and it required the constant use of the bellows to keep in a sufficient quantity of air. For a long time we scarcely seemed to approach our island, but gradually we worked across the rougher sea of the open channel, into the smoother water under the lee of the island, and began to discover that what we took for a long row of pelicans, ranged on the beach, were only low cliffs whitened with salt by the spray of the waves: and about noon we reached the shore, the transparency of the water enabling us to see the bottom at a considerable depth.

"The cliffs and masses of rock along the shore were whitened by an incrustation of salt where the waves dashed up against them; and the evaporating water, which had been left in holes and hollows on the surface of the rocks, was covered with a crust of salt about one-eighth of an inch in thickness.

"Carrying with us the barometer and other instruments, in the afternoon we ascended to the highest point of the island—a bare, rocky peak, 800 feet above the lake. Standing on the summit, we enjoyed an extended view of the lake, enclosed in a basin of rugged mountains, which sometimes left marshy flats and extensive bottoms between them and the shore and in other places came directly down into the water with bold and precipitous bluffs.

"As we looked over the vast expanse of water spread out beneath us, and strained our eyes along the silent shores over which hung so much doubt and uncertainty, and which were so full of interest to us, I could hardly repress the almost irresistible desire to continue our exploration; but the lengthening snow on the mountains was a plain indication of the advancing season, and our frail linen boat appeared so insecure that I was unwilling to trust our lives to the uncertainties of the lake. I therefore unwillingly resolved to terminate our survey here, and remain satisfied for the present with what we had been able to add to the unknown geography of the region. We felt pleasure also in remembering that we were the first who, in the traditionary annals of the country, had visited the islands, and broken, with the cheerful sound of human voices, the long solitude of the place.

"I accidentally left on the summit the brass cover to the object end of my spy-glass; and as it will probably remain there undisturbed by Indians, it will furnish matter of speculation to some future traveler. In our excursions about the island, we did not meet with any kind of animal; a magpie, and another larger bird, probably attracted by the smoke of our fire, paid us a visit from the shore, and were the only living things seen during our stay. The rock constituting the cliffs along the shore where we were encamped, is a talcous rock, or steatite, with brown spar.

"At sunset, the temperature was 70°. We

had arrived just in time to obtain a meridian altitude of the sun, and other observations were obtained this evening, which place our camp in latitude 41° 10' 42", and longtitude 112° 21' 05" from Greenwich. From a discussion of the barometrical observations made during our stay on the shores of the lake, we have adopted 4,200 feet for its elevation above the Gulf of Mexico. In the first disappointment we felt from the dissipation of our dream of the fertile islands, I called this Disappointment Island.

"Out of the driftwood we made ourselves pleasant little lodges, open to the water, and, after having kindled large fires to excite the wonder of any straggling savage on the lake shores, lay down, for the first time in a long journey, in perfect security; no one thinking about his arms. The evening was extremely bright and pleasant; but the wind rose during the night, and the waves began to break heavily on the shore, making our island tremble. I had not expected in our inland journey to hear the roar of an ocean surf; and the strangeness of our situation, and the excitement we felt in the associated interests of the place, made this one of the most interesting nights I remember during our long expedition.

"In the morning, the surf was breaking heavily on the shore, and we were up early. The lake was dark and agitated, and we hurried through our scanty breakfast, and embarked— having first filled one of the buckets with water from which it was intended to make salt. The sun had risen by the time we were ready to start; and it was blowing a strong gale of wind, almost directly off the shore, and raising a considerable sea, in which our boat strained very much. It roughened as we got away from the island, and it required all the efforts of the men to make any head against the wind of the sea; the gale rising with the sun; and there was danger of being blown into one of the open reaches beyond the island. At the distance of half a mile from the beach, the depth of water was sixteen feet, with a clay bottom; but, as the working of the boat was very severe labor, and during the operation of sounding, it was necessary to cease paddling, during which the boat lost considerable way, I was unwilling to discourage the men, and reluctantly gave up my intention of ascertaining the depth and character of the bed. There was a general shout in the boat when we found ourselves in one fathom, and we soon after landed on a low point of mud, where we unloaded the boat, and carried the baggage to firmer ground."

Roughly evaporated over the fire, the five gallons of water from this lake yielded fourteen pints of very fine-grained and very white salt, of which the whole lake may be regarded as a saturated solution.

On the 12th they resumed their journey, returning by the same route, and at night had a supper of sea-gulls, which Carson killed near the lake.

The next day they continued up the river, hunger making them very quiet and peaceable, and there was rarely an oath to be heard in the camp—not even a solitary *enfant de garce*. It was time for the men with an expected supply of provisions from Fitzpatrick to be in the neighborhood; and the gun was fired at evening, to give notice of their locality, but met with no response.

They killed to-day a fat young horse, purchased from the Indians, and were very soon restored to gaiety and good humor. Fremont and Mr. Preuss, not having yet overcome the prejudices of civilization, did not partake, preferring to turn in supperless.

The large number of emigrants constantly

encamping here had driven the game into the mountains, so that not an elk or antelope was seen upon the route; but an antelope was purchased from an Indian, for a little powder and some ball, and they encamped early to enjoy an abundant supper; which, while not yet prepared, was interrupted by the arrival of a trapper, who startled and rejoiced all by announcing the glad news, that Mr. Fitzpatrick was in camp a little way from them, with a plentiful supply of provisions, flour, rice, dried meat, and even butter.

CHAPTER XXI.

The difficulty, in view of the approaching winter season, of supporting a large party, determined Fremont to send back a number of the men who had become satisfied that they were not fitted for the laborious service and frequent privation to which they were necessarily exposed, and which there was reason to believe would become more severe in the further extension of the voyage. They were accordingly called together, and after being fully informed as to the nature of the duties imposed upon them, and the hardships they would have to undergo, eleven of the party consented to abandon Fremont, and return; but Carson was not one of these.

Taking leave of the homeward party, they resumed their journey down the valley, the weather being very cold, and the rain coming in hard gusts, which the wind blew directly in their faces. They forded the Portneuf in a storm of rain, the water in the river being frequently up to the axles.

Fremont in his official report thus enumerates some of the difficulties and sufferings the party had to encounter:

"*September* 27.—It was now no longer possible, as in our previous journey, to travel regularly every day, and find at any moment a convenient place for repose at noon, or a camp at night; but the halting places were now generally fixed along the road, by the nature of the country, at places where, with water, there was a little scanty grass. Since leaving the American falls, the road had frequently been very bad; and many short, steep ascents exhausting the strength of our worn-out animals, requiring always at such places the assistance of the men to get up each cart, one by one; and our progress with twelve or fourteen wheeled carriages, though light and made for the purpose, in such a rocky country, was extremely slow.

"Carson had met here three or four buffalo bulls, two of which were killed. They were among the pioneers which had made the experiment of colonizing in the valley of the Columbia.

"Opposite to the encampment, a subterranean river bursts out directly from the face of the escarpment, and falls in white foam to the river below. The main river is enclosed with mural precipices, which form its characteristic feature, along a great portion of its course. A melancholy and strange-looking country—one of fracture, and violence, and fire.

"We had brought with us when we separated from the camp a large gaunt ox, in appearance very poor; but, being killed to-night, to the great joy of the people, he was found to be remarkably fat. As usual at such occurrences, the evening was devoted to gaiety and feasting; abundant fare now made an epoch among us; and in this laborious life, in such a country as this, our men had but little else to enjoy."

On arriving at the ford where the road crosses to the right bank of Snake River, an Indian was hired to conduct them through the ford, which proved impracticable; the water sweeping away the howitzer and nearly drowning the mules. Fortunately they had a resource in a boat, which was filled with air and launched; and at seven o'clock were safely encamped on the opposite bank, the animals swimming across, and the carriage, howitzer, and baggage of the camp being carried over in the boat.

It was while at Fort Boise where Fremont first met Mons. Payette, an employee of the Hudson Bay Co., that he came across the "Fish-eating Indians," a class lower if possible in the scale of humanity than the "Diggers." He says

"Many little accounts and scattered histories, together with an acquaintance which I gradually acquired of their modes of life, had left the aboriginal inhabitants of this vast region pictured in my mind as a race of people whose great and constant occupation was the means of procuring a subsistence.

"While the summer weather and the salmon lasted, they lived contentedly and happily, scattered along the different streams where the fish were to be found; and as soon as the winter snows began to fall, little smokes would be seen rising among the mountains, where they would be found in miserable groups, starving out the winter; and sometimes, according to the general belief, reduced to the horror of cannibalism—the strong, of course, preying on the weak. Certain it is, they are driven to an extremity for food, and eat every insect, and every creeping thing, however loathsome and repulsive. Snails, lizards, ants—all are devoured with the readiness and greediness of mere animals."

The remainder of the overland journey, until they reached Nez Percé, one of the trading establishments of the Hudson Bay Company, was not marked by any incident bringing Carson into special notice.

Having now completed the connection of his explorations with those of Commander Wilkes, and which was the limit of his instructions, Fremont commenced preparations for his return, Carson being left at the *Dalles* with directions to occupy the people in making packsaddles, and refitting the equipage; while Fremont continued his journey to the Mission, a few miles down the Columbia River, where he passed a few days in comparative luxury.

The few days of rest, added to an abundance of wholesome food, had so far recruited the party, that they were soon prepared to encounter and conquer the difficulties of this overland journey in mid-winter. Three principal objects were indicated by Fremont for exploration and research, and which, despite the obstacles which the season must so surely interpose, he had determined to visit.

The first of these points was the *Tlamath*

Lake, on the table-land between the head of Fall River, which comes to the Columbia, and the Sacramento, which goes to the bay of San Francisco ; and from which lake a river of the same name makes its way westwardly direct to the ocean.

From this lake their course was intended to be about southeast, to a reported lake called Mary's, at some days' journey in the Great Basin ; and thence, still on southeast, to the reputed *Buenaventura* River, which has had a place in so many maps, and countenanced the belief of the existence of a great river flowing from the Rocky Mountains to the bay of San Francisco. From the Buenaventura, the next point was intended to be in that section of the Rocky Mountains which includes the heads of Arkansas River, and of the opposite waters of the Californian Gulf ; and thence down the Arkansas to Bent's Fort, and home. This was the projected line of return—a great part of it absolutely new to geographical, botanical, and geological science—and the subject of reports in relation to lakes, rivers, deserts, and savages, hardly above the condition of mere wild animals, which inflamed desire to know what this *terra incognita* really contained.

It was a serious enterprise at the commencement of winter to undertake the traverse of such a region, and with a party consisting only of twenty-five persons, and they of many nations —American, French, German, Canadian, Indian, and colored—and most of them young, several being under twenty-one years of age. All knew that a strange country was to be explored, and dangers and hardships to be encountered; but no one blenched at the prospect. On the contrary, courage and confidence animated the whole party. Cheerfulness, readiness, subordination, prompt obedience, characterized all; nor did any extremity of peril and privation, to which they were afterwards exposed, ever belie, or derogate from, the fine spirit of this brave and generous commencement.

For the support of the party, he had provided at Vancouver a supply of provisions for not less than three months, consisting principally of flour, peas, and tallow—the latter being used in cooking; and, in addition to this, they had purchased at the mission some California cattle, which were to be driven on the hoof. They had one hundred and four mules and horses—part of the latter procured from the

Indians about the mission; and for the sustenance of which, their reliance was upon the grass which might be found, and the soft porous wood, which was to be substituted when there was no grass.

Mr. Fitzpatrick, with Mr. Talbot and the remainder of the party, arrived on the 21st; and the camp was now closely engaged in the labor of preparation. Mr. Perkins succeeded in obtaining as a guide, to the Tlamath Lake, two Indians—one of whom had been there, and bore the marks of several wounds he had received from some of the Indians in the neighborhood.

Tlamath Lake, however, on examination, proved to be simply a shallow basin, which for a short period of the time of melting snows, is covered with water from the neighboring mountains; but this probably soon runs off, and leaves for the remainder of the year a green savannah, through the midst of which the river Tlamath, which flows to the ocean, winds its way to the outlet on the southwestern side.

After leaving Tlamath Lake the party headed for Mary's Lake, which, however, after incredible sufferings and hardships, they failed to discover, but they found one which was appropriately christened "Pyramid Lake," and here the record of toils, dangers and sufferings, undergone by the whole party, can only be told in the language of him, who cheerfully toiled and suffered with those under his command, and it is not too much to say, that with the exception of the "Strain expedition," across the Isthmus of Darien, no party of men have ever lived to narrate such sad experiences. We therefore let Fremont, in his own modest way, tell the tale of his own and his companions' sufferings.

CHAPTER XXII.

"*January* 3.—A fog, so dense that we could not see a hundred yards, covered the country, and the men that were sent out after the horses were bewildered and lost; and we were consequently detained at camp until late in the day. Our situation had now become a serious one. We had reached and run over the position where, according to the best maps in my possession, we should have found Mary's Lake or river. We were evidently on the verge of the desert which had been reported to us; and the appearance of the country was so forbidding, that I was afraid to enter it, and determined to bear away to the southward, keeping close along the mountains, in the full expectation of reaching the Buenaventura River. This morning I put every man in the camp on foot—myself, of course, among the rest—and in this manner lightened by distribution the loads of the animals.

"*January* 4.—The fog to-day was still more

dense, and the people again were bewildered. We traveled a few miles around the western point of the ridge, and encamped where there were a few tufts of grass, but no water. Our animals now were in a very alarming state, and there was increasing anxiety in the camp.

"*January* 5.—Same dense fog continued, and one of the mules died in camp this morning. We moved to a place where there was a little better grass, about two miles distant. Taplin, one of our best men, who had gone out on a scouting excursion, ascended a mountain near by, and to his great surprise emerged into a region of bright sunshine, in which the upper parts of the mountain were glowing, while below all was obscured in the darkest fog.

"*January* 6.—The fog continued the same, and with Mr. Preuss and Carson, I ascended the mountain, to sketch the leading features of the country, as some indication of our future route, while Mr. Fitzpatrick explored the country below. In a very short distance we had ascended above the mist, but the view obtained was not very gratifying. The fog had partially cleared off from below when we reached the summit; and in the southwest corner of a basin communicating with that in which we had encamped, we saw a lofty column of smoke, 16 miles distant, indicating the presence of hot springs. There, also, appeared to be the outlet of those draining channels of the country; and, as such places afforded always more or less grass, I determined to steer in that direction. The ridge we had ascended appeared to be composed of fragments of white granite. We saw here traces of sheep and antelope.

"Entering the neighboring valley, and crossing the bed of another lake, after a hard day's travel over ground of yielding mud and sand, we reached the springs, where we found an abundance of grass, which, though only tolerably good, made this place, with reference to the past, a refreshing and agreeable spot.

"This is the most extraordinary locality of hot springs we had met during the journey. The basin of the largest one has a circumference of several hundred feet; but there is at one extremity a circular space of about fifteen feet in diameter, entirely occupied by the boiling water. It boils up at irregular intervals, and with much noise. The water is clear, and the spring deep; a pole about sixteen feet long was easily immersed in the center, but we had no means of forming a good idea of the depth.

"Taking with me Godey and Carson. I made to-day a thorough exploration of the neighboring valleys, and found in a ravine in the bordering mountains a good camping place, where was water in springs, and a sufficient quantity of grass for a night. Overshadowing the springs were some trees of the sweet cotton-wood, which, after a long interval of absence, we saw again with pleasure, regarding them as harbingers of a better country. To us, they were eloquent of green prairies and buffalo. We found here a broad and plainly marked trail, on which there were tracks of horses, and we appeared to have regained one of the thoroughfares which pass by the watering places of the country. On the western mountains of the valley, with which this of the boiling spring communicates, we remarked scattered cedars—probably an indication that we were on the borders of the timbered region extending to the Pacific. We reached the camp at sunset, after a day's ride of about forty miles.

"*January* 10.—We continued our reconnoissance ahead, pursuing a south direction in the basin along the ridge; the camp following slowly after. On a large trail there is never any doubt of finding suitable places for encampments. We reached the end of the basin, where we found, in a hollow of the mountain which enclosed it, an abundance of good bunch grass. Leaving a signal for the party to encamp, we continued our way up the hollow, intending to see what lay beyond the mountain. The hollow was several miles long, forming a good pass, the snow deepening to about a foot as we neared the summit. Beyond, a defile between the mountains descended rapidly about two thousand feet; and, filling up all the lower space, was a sheet of green water, some twenty miles broad. It broke upon our eyes like the ocean. The neighboring peaks rose high above us, and we ascended one of them to obtain a better view. The waves were curling in the breeze, and their dark green color showed it to be a body of deep water. For a long time we sat enjoying the view, for we had become fatigued with mountains, and the free expanse of moving waves was very grateful. It was set like a gem in the mountains, which, from our position, seemed to enclose it almost entirely. At the western end it communicated with the line of basins we had left a few days since; and on the opposite side it swept a ridge of snowy mountains, the foot of the great Sierra. Its position at first inclined us to believe it Mary's Lake, but the rugged mountains were so entirely discordant with descriptions of its low rushy shores and open country, that we concluded it some unknown body of water; which it afterwards proved to be.

"We saw before us, in descending from the pass, a great continuous range, along which stretched the valley of the river; the lower parts steep, and dark with pines, while above it was hidden in clouds of snow. This, we felt instantly satisfied, was the central ridge of the Sierra Nevada, the great California mountain, which only now intervened between us and the waters of the bay. We had made a forced march of 26 miles, and three mules had given out on the road. Up to this point, with the exception of two stolen by Indians, we had lost none of the horses which had been brought from the Columbia River, and a number of these were still strong and in tolerably good order. We had now sixty-seven animals in the band.

"We had scarcely lighted our fires, when the camp was crowded with nearly naked Indians. There were two who appeared particularly intelligent—one, a somewhat old man. He told me that, before the snows fell, it was six sleeps

to the place where the whites lived, but that
now it was impossible to cross the mountain on
account of the deep snow; and showing us, as
the others had done, that it was over our
heads, he urged us strongly to follow the
course of the river, which he said would conduct us to a lake in which there were many
large fish. There, he said, were many people;
there was no snow on the ground; and we
might remain there until spring. From their
descriptions, we were enabled to judge that we
had encamped on the upper water of the Sal-
mon-trout River. It is hardly necessary to
say that our communication was only by signs,
as we understood nothing of their language;
but they spoke, notwithstanding, rapidly and
vehemently, explaining what they considered
the folly of our intentions, and urging us to go
down to the lake. *Tah-ve*, a word signifying
snow, we very soon learned to know, from its
frequent repetition. I told him that the men
and the horses were strong, and that we would
break a road through the snow; and spreading
before him our bales of scarlet cloth and trinkets, showed him what we would give for a
guide. It was necessary to obtain one, if possible; for I had determined here to attempt

the passage of the mountain. Pulling a bunch of grass from the ground, after a short discussion among themselves, the old man made us comprehend, that if we could break through the snow, at the end of three days we would come down upon grass, which he showed us would be about six inches high, and where the ground was entirely free. So far he said he had been in hunting for elk ; but beyond that (and he closed his eyes) he had seen nothing ; but there was one among them who had been to the whites, and, going out of the lodge, he returned with a young man of very intelligent appearance. Here, said he, is a young man who has seen the whites with his own eyes ; and he swore, first by the sky, and then by the ground, that what he said was true. With a large present of goods, we prevailed upon this young man to be our guide, and he acquired among us the name Mélo—a word signifying friend, which they used very frequently. He was thinly clad, and nearly barefoot; his moccasins being about worn out. We gave him skins to make a new pair, and to enable him to perform his undertaking to us. The Indians remained in camp during the night, and we kept the guide and two others to sleep in the lodge with us—

Carson lying across the door, and having made them comprehend the use of our firearms."

Fremont here, after a consultation with some Indians who came into his camp, made up his mind to attempt the passage of the mountains at every hazard. He therefore, to quote his own words, called his men together, and "reminded them of the beautiful valley of the Sacramento, with which they were familiar from the descriptions of Carson, who had been there some fifteen years ago, and who, in our late privations, had delighted us in speaking of its rich pastures and abundant game, and drew a vivid contrast between its summer climate, less than a hundred miles distant, and the falling snow around us. I informed them (and long experience had given them confidence in my observations and good instruments) that almost directly west, and only about seventy miles distant, was the great farming establishment of Captain Sutter—a gentleman who had formerly lived in Missouri, and, emigrating to this country, had become the possessor of a principality. I assured them that, from the heights of the mountain before us, we should doubtless see the valley of the Sacramento River, and with one effort place ourselves again in the midst of plenty. The people received this decision with the cheerful obedience which had always characterized them; and the day was immediately devoted to the preparations necessary to enable us to carry it into effect. Leggins, moccasins, clothing—all were put into the best state to resist the cold. Our guide was not neglected. Extremity of suffering might make him desert; we therefore did the best we could for him. Leggins, moccasins, some articles of clothing, and a large green blanket, in addition to the blue and scarlet cloth, were lavished upon him, and to his great and evident contentment. He arrayed himself in all his colors; and clad in green, blue, and scarlet, he made a gay-looking Indian; and, with his various presents, was probably richer and better clothed than any of his tribe had ever been before.

"I have already said that our provisions were very low; we had neither tallow nor grease of any kind remaining, and the want of salt became one of our greatest privations. The poor dog which had been found in the Bear River valley, and which had been a *compagnon de voyage* ever since, had now become fat, and the mess to which it belonged requested permission to kill it. Leave was granted. Spread out on the snow, the meat looked very good; and it made a strengthening meal for the greater part of the camp.

"The people were unusually silent; for every man knew that our enterprise was hazardous, and the issue doubtful.

"The snow deepened rapidly, and it soon became necessary to break a road. For this service, a party of ten was formed, mounted on the strongest horses; each man in succession opening the road on foot, or on horseback, until himself and his horse became fatigued, when he stepped aside; and, the remaining number passing ahead, he took his station in the rear.

"The camp had been all the day occupied in endeavoring to ascend the hill, but only the best horses had succeeded; the animals, generally, not having sufficient strength to bring themselves up without the packs; and all the line of road between this and the springs was strewed with camp stores and equipage, and horses floundering in snow. I therefore immediately encamped on the ground with my own mess, which was in advance, and directed Mr. Fitzpatrick to encamp at the springs, and send all the animals, in charge of Tabeau, with a strong guard, back to the place where they had been pastured the night before. Here was a small spot of level ground, protected on one side by the mountain, and on the other sheltered by a little ridge of rock. It was an open grove of pines, which assimilated in size to the grandeur of the mountain, being frequently six feet in diameter.

"To-night we had no shelter, but we made a large fire around the trunk of one of the huge pines; and covering the snow with small boughs, on which we spread our blankets, soon made ourselves comfortable. The night was very bright and clear, though the thermometer was only at 10°. A strong wind which sprang up at sundown made it intensely cold; and this was one of the bitterest nights during the journey.

"Two Indians joined our party here; and one of them, an old man, immediately began to harangue us, saying that ourselves and animals would perish in the snow; and that, if we would go back, he would show us another and a better way across the mountain. He spoke in a very loud voice, and there was a singular repetition of phrases and arrangement of words, which rendered his speech striking, and not unmusical.

"We had now begun to understand some

words, and, with the aid of signs, easily comprehended the old man's simple ideas. 'Rock upon rock—rock upon rock—snow upon snow —snow upon snow,' said he; 'even if you get over the snow, you will not be able to get down from the mountains.' He made us the sign of precipices, and showed us how the feet of the horses would slip, and throw them off from the narrow trails which led along their sides. Our Chinook, who comprehended even more readily than ourselves, and believed our situation hopeless, covered his head with his blanket, and began to weep and lament. 'I wanted to see the whites,' said he; 'I came away from my own people to see the whites, and I wouldn't care to die among them; but here'—and he looked around into the cold night and gloomy forest, and, drawing his blanket over his head, began again to lament.

"Seated around the tree, the fire illuminating the rocks and the tall bolls of the pines round about, and the old Indian haranguing, we presented a group of very serious faces.

"*February* 5.—The night had been too cold to sleep, and we were up very early. Our guide was standing by the fire with all his finery on; and seeing him shiver in the cold, I threw on his shoulders one of my blankets. We missed him a few minutes afterwards, and never saw him again. He had deserted. His bad faith and treachery were in perfect keeping with the estimate of Indian character, which a long intercourse with this people had gradually forced upon my mind.

"While a portion of the camp were occupied in bringing up the baggage to this point, the remainder were busied in making sledges and snow-shoes. I had determined to explore the mountain ahead, and the sledges were to be used in transporting the baggage.

"Crossing the open basin, in a march of about ten miles we reached the top of one of the peaks, to the left of the pass indicated by our guide. Far below us, dimmed by the distance, was a large, snowless valley, bounded on the western side, at the distance of about a hundred miles, by a low range of mountains, which Carson recognized with delight as the mountains bordering the coast. 'There,' said he, 'is the little mountain—it is fifteen years ago since I saw it; but I am just as sure as if I had seen it yesterday.' Between us, then, and this low coast range, was the valley of the Sacramento; and no one who had not accompanied us through the incidents of our life for the last few months, could realize the delight with which at last we looked down upon it. At the distance of apparently thirty miles beyond us were distinguished spots of prairie; and a dark line, which could be traced with the glass, was imagined to be the course of the river; but we were evidently at a great height above the valley, and between us and the plains extended miles of snowy fields and broken ridges of pine-covered mountains.

"It was late in the day when we turned towards the camp; and it grew rapidly cold as it drew towards night. One of the men became fatigued, and his feet began to freeze, and building a fire in the trunk of a dry old cedar, Mr. Fitzpatrick remained with him until his clothes could be dried, and he was in a condition to come on. After a day's march of twenty miles, we straggled into camp, one after another, at nightfall; the greater number excessively fatigued, only two of the party having ever traveled on snow-shoes before.

"All our energies were now directed to getting our animals across the snow; and it was supposed that, after all the baggage had been drawn with the sleighs over the trail we had made, it would be sufficiently hard to bear our animals.

"At several places, between this point and the ridge, we had discovered some grassy spots, where the wind and sun had dispersed the snow from the sides of the hills, and these were to form resting places to support the animals for a night in their passage across. On our way across, we had set on fire several broken stumps and dried trees, to melt holes in the snow for the camp. Its general depth was five feet; but we passed over places where it was twenty feet deep, as shown by the trees.

"With one party drawing sleighs loaded with baggage, I advanced to-day about four miles along the trail, and encamped at the first grassy spot, where we expected to bring our horses. Mr. Fitzpatrick, with another party, remained behind, to form an intermediate station between us and the animals.

"Putting on our snow-shoes, we spent the afternoon in exploring a road ahead. The glare of the snow, combined with great fatigue, had rendered many of the people nearly blind; but we were fortunate in having some black silk handkerchiefs, which, worn as veils, very much relieved the eye.

" In the evening I received a message from Mr Fitzpatrick, acquainting me with the utter failure of his attempt to get our mules and horses over the snow—the half-hidden trail had proved entirely too slight to support them, and they had broken through, and were plunging about or lying half buried in snow. He was occupied in endeavoring to get them back to his camp; and in the mean time sent to me for further instructions. I wrote to him to send the animals immediately back to their old pastures; and, after having made mauls and shovels, turn in all the strength of his party to open and beat a road through the snow, strengthening it with branches and boughs of the pines.

"*February* 12.—We made mauls, and worked hard at our end of the road all the day. The wind was high, but the sun bright, and the snow thawing. We worked down the face of the hill, to meet the people at the other end. Towards sundown it began to grow cold, and we shouldered our mauls, and trudged back to camp.

"*February* 13.—We continued to labor on the road; and in the course of the day had the satisfaction to see the people working down the face of the opposite hill, about three miles distant. During the morning we had the pleasure of a visit from Mr. Fitzpatrick, with the information that all was going on well. A party of Indians had passed on snow-shoes, who said they were going to the western side of the mountain after fish. This was an indication that the salmon were coming up the streams; and we could hardly restrain our impatience as we thought of them, and worked with increased vigor.

"I was now perfectly satisfied that we had struck the stream on which Mr. Sutter lived, and turning about, made a hard push, and reached the camp at dark. Here we had the pleasure to find all the remaining animals, 57 in number, safely arrived at the grassy hill near the camp; and here, also, we were agreeably surprised with the sight of an abundance of salt. Some of the horse guard had gone to a neighboring hut for pine nuts, and discovered unexpectedly a large cake of very white fine-grained salt, which the Indians told them they had brought from the other side of the mountain; they used it to eat with their pine nuts, and readily sold it for goods.

"On the 19th, the people were occupied in making a road and bringing up the baggage;

and, on the afternoon of the next day, *February* 20, 1844, we encamped with the animals and all the *materiel* of the camp, on the summit of the Pass in the dividing ridge, 1,000 miles by our traveled road from the Dalles of the Columbia.

"*February* 21.—We now considered ourselves victorious over the mountain; having only the descent before us, and the valley under our eyes, we felt strong hope that we should force our way down. But this was a case in which the descent was *not* facile. Still, deep delds of snow lay between, and there was a large intervening space of rough-looking mountains, through which we had yet to wind our way. Carson roused me this morning with an early fire, and we were all up long before day, in order to pass the snow fields before the sun should render the crust soft. We enjoyed this morning a scene at sunrise, which, even here, was unusually glorious and beautiful. Immediately above the eastern mountains was repeated a cloud-formed mass of purple ranges, bordered with bright yellow gold; the peaks shot up into a narrow line of crimson cloud, above which the air was filled with a greenish orange; and over all was the singular beauty of the blue sky. Passing along a ridge which commanded the lake on our right, of which we began to discover an outlet through a chasm on the west, we passed over alternating open ground and hard-crusted snow-fields which supported the animals, and encamped on the ridge after a journey of six miles. The grass was better than we had yet seen, and we were encamped in a clump of trees, twenty or thirty feet high, resembling white pine.

CHAPTER XXIII.

"We had hard and doubtful labor yet before us, as the snow appeared to be heavier where the timber began further down, with few open spots. Ascending a height, we traced out the best line we could discover for the next day's march, and had at least the consolation to see that the mountain descended rapidly. The day had been one of April; gusty, with a few occasional flakes of snow; which, in the afternoon, enveloped the upper mountains in clouds. We watched them anxiously, as now we dreaded a snow-storm. Shortly afterwards we heard the roll of thunder, and looking toward the valley, found it all enveloped in a thunder-storm. For us, as connected with the idea of summer, it had a singular charm; and we watched its progress with excited feelings until nearly sunset, when the sky cleared off brightly, and we saw a shining line of water directing its course towards another, a broader and larger sheet. We knew that these could be no other than the Sacramento and the bay of San Francisco; but, after our long wandering in rugged mountains, where so frequently we had met with disappointment, and where the crossing of every ridge displayed some unknown lake or river, we were yet almost afraid to believe that we were at last to escape into the genial country of which we have heard so many glowing descriptions, and dreaded again to find some vast interior lake, whose bitter waters would bring us disappointments. On the southern shore of what appeared to be the bay, could be traced the gleaming line where entered another large stream; and again the Buenaventura rose up in our mind.

"Carson had entered the valley along the southern side of the bay, but the country then was so entirely covered with water from snow and rain, that he had been able to form no correct impression of watercourses.

"We had the satisfaction to know that at least there were people below. Fires were lit up in the valley just at night, appearing to be in answer to ours; and these signs of life renewed, in some measure, the gaiety of the camp. They appeared so near, that we judged them to be among the timber of some of the neighboring ridges; but, having them constantly in view day after day, and night after night, we afterwards found them to be fires that had been kindled by the Indians among the *tulares*, on the shore of the bay, eighty miles distant.

"Axes and mauls were necessary to-day to make a road through the snow. Going ahead with Carson to reconnoiter the road, we reached in the afternoon the river which made the outlet of the lake. Carson sprang over, clear across a place where the stream was compressed among rocks, but the *parfleche* sole of my moccasin glanced from the icy rock, and precipitated me into the river. It was some few seconds before I could recover myself in the current, and Carson, thinking me hurt, jumped in after me, and we both had an icy bath. We tried to search a while for my gun, which had been lost in the fall, but the cold drove us out; and making a large fire on the bank, after we had partially dried ourselves we went back to meet the camp. We afterwards found that the gun had been slung under the ice which lined the banks of the creek.

"The sky was clear and pure, with a sharp wind from the northeast, and the thermometer 2° below the freezing point.

"We continued down the south face of the

mountain; our road leading over dry ground, we were able to avoid the snow almost entirely In the course of the morning, we struck a footpath, which we were generally able to keep and the ground was soft to our animals' feet, being sandy or covered with mold. Green grass began to make its appearance, and occasionally we passed a hill scatteringly covered with it. The character of the forest continued the same; and, among the trees, the pine with sharp leaves and very large cones was abundant, some of them being noble trees. We measured one that had ten feet diameter, though the height was not more than one hundred and thirty feet. All along, the river was a roaring torrent, its fall very great; and, descending with a rapidity to which we had long been strangers to our great pleasure oak trees appeared on the ridge, and soon became very frequent; on these I remarked unusually great quantities of mistletoe.

"The opposite mountain side was very steep and continuous—unbroken by ravines, and covered with pines and snow; while on the side we were traveling, innumerable rivulets poured down from the ridge. Continuing on, we halted a moment at one of these rivulets, to ad mire some beautiful evergreen trees, resembling live oak, which shaded the little stream. They were forty to fifty feet high, and two in diameter, with a uniform tufted top; and the summer green of their beautiful foliage, with the singing birds, and the sweet summer wind which was whirling about the dry oak leaves, nearly intoxicated us with delight; and we hurried on, filled with excitement, to escape entirely from the horrid region of inhospitable snow, to the perpetual spring of the Sacramento.

"*February* 25.—Believing that the difficulties of the road were passed, and leaving Mr. Fitzpatrick to follow slowly, as the condition of the animals required, I started ahead this morning with a party of eight, consisting (with myself) of Mr. Preuss, and Mr. Talbot, Carson, Derosier, Towns, Proue, and Jacob. We took with us some of the best animals, and my intention was to proceed as rapidly as possible to the house of Mr. Sutter, and return to meet the party with a supply of provisions and fresh animals.

"Near nightfall we descended into the steep ravine of a handsome creek thirty feet wide, and I was engaged in getting the horses up the opposite hill, when I heard a shout from Carson, who had gone ahead a few hundred yards—'Life yet,' said he, as he came up, 'life yet; I have found a hillside sprinkled with grass enough for the night.' We drove along our horses, and encamped at the place about dark, and there was just room enough to make a place for shelter on the edge of the stream. Three horses were lost to-day—Proveau; a fine young horse from the Columbia belonging to Charles Towns; and another Indian horse which carried our cooking utensils; the two former gave out, and the latter strayed off into the woods as we reached the camp: and Derosier, knowing my attachment to Proveau, volunteered to go and bring him in.

"Carson and I climbed one of the nearest mountains; the forest land still extended ahead, and the valley appeared as far as ever. The pack-horse was found near the camp, but De rosier did not get in.

"We began to be uneasy at Derosier's absence, fearing he might have been bewildered in the woods. Charles Towns, who had not yet recovered his mind, went to swim in the river, as if it was summer, and the stream placid, when it was a cold mountain torrent foaming among the rocks. We were happy to see Derosier appear in the evening. He came in, and sitting down

by the fire, began to tell us where he had been.
He imagined he had been gone several days, and
thought we were still at the camp where he had
left us; and we were pained to see that his
mind was deranged. It appeared that he had
been lost in the mountain, and hunger and
fatigue, joined to weakness of body, and fear of
perishing in the mountains had crazed him. The
times were severe when stout men lost their
minds from extremity of suffering,—when horses
died—and when mules and horses, ready to die
of starvation, were killed for food. Yet there
was no murmuring or hesitation. In the mean
time Mr. Preuss continued on down the river,
and unaware that we had encamped so early in
the day, was lost. When night arrived and he
did not come in, we began to understand what
had happened to him; but it was too late to
make any search.

"*March* 3.—We followed Mr. Preuss's trail
for a considerable distance along the river, until we reached a place where he had descended
to the stream below and encamped. Here we
shouted and fired guns, but received no answer;
and we concluded that he had pushed on down
the stream. I determined to keep out from the
river, along which it was nearly impracticable

to travel with animals, until it should form a valley. At every step the country improved in beauty; the pines were rapidly disappearing, and oaks became the principal trees of the forest. Among these, the prevailing tree was the evergreen oak (which, by way of distinction, we shall call the *live* oak); and with these, occurred frequently a new species of oak, bearing a long, slender acorn, from an inch to an inch and a half in length, which we now began to see formed the principal vegetable food of the inhabitants of this region. In a short distance we crossed a little rivulet, where were two old huts, and near by were heaps of acorn hulls. The ground round about was very rich, covered with an exuberant sward of grass; and we sat down for a while in the shade of the oaks, to let the animals feed. We repeated our shouts for Mr. Preuss ; and this time we were gratified with an answer. The voice grew rapidly nearer, ascending from the river, but when we expected to see him emerge, it ceased entirely. We had called up some straggling Indian—the first we had met, although for two days back we had seen tracks—who, mistaking us for his fellows, had been only undeceived by getting close up. It would have been pleas ant to witness his astonishment; he would not have been more frightened had some of the old mountain spirits they are so much afraid of suddenly appeared in his path. Ignorant of the character of these people, we had now additional cause of uneasiness in regard to Mr. Preuss; he had no arms with him, and we began to think his chance doubtful. Occasionally we met deer, but had not the necessary time for hunting. At one of these orchard grounds, we encamped about noon to make an effort for Mr. Preuss. One man took his way along a spur leading into the river, in hope to cross his trail; and another took our own back. Both were volunteers; and to the successful man was promised a pair of pistols—not as a reward, but as a token of gratitude for a service which would free us all from much anxiety."

It was not until the 6th, and after a continuation of the most incredible sufferings, already narrated, that the party reached Sutter's Fort, where, it is needless to say, they were warmly and cordially received by that gentleman,—and to close this stirring narrative, we will only add, as an evidence of the terrible sufferings to which they had been subjected, that out of sixty-seven horses and mules, with which the expedition was commenced, only thirty-three reached the valley of the Sacramento, and they had to be led. In quoting above from Fremont's narrative, a continuous record has not been kept, as we have used only such portions as contain the narrative of incidents directly connected with the expedition, and of which, though scarcely mentioned throughout, save in the most incidental manner, Carson might well say, and with pride, *magna pars fui*.

In the course of this narrative we have frequently used the word *cache*, and a brief interpretation of its meaning, we are sure, will not be uninteresting to the uninitiated.

A cache is a term common among traders and hunters, to designate a hiding place for provisions and effects. It is derived from the French word *cacher*, to conceal, and originated among the early colonists of Canada and Louisiana; but the secret depository which it designates was in use among the aboriginals long before the intrusion of the white men. It is, in fact, the only mode that migratory hordes have of preserving their valuables from robbery, during their long absences from their villages or accustomed haunts on hunting expeditions, or during the vicissitudes of war. The utmost skill and caution are required to render these places of concealment invisible to the lynx eye of an Indian.

The first care is to seek out a proper situation, which is generally some dry low bank of clay, on the margin of a water-course. As soon as the precise spot is pitched upon, blankets, saddle-cloths, and other coverings are spread over the surrounding grass and bushes, to prevent foot tracks, or any other derangement; and as few hands as possible are employed. A circle of about two feet in diameter is then nicely cut in the sod, which is carefully removed, with the loose soil immediately beneath it, and laid aside in a place where it will be safe from anything that may change its appearance. The uncovered area is then digged perpendicularly to the depth of about three feet, and is then gradually widened so as to form a conical chamber six or seven feet deep.

The whole of the earth displaced by this process, being of a different color from that on the surface, is handed up in a vessel, and heaped into a skin or cloth, in which it is conveyed to the stream and thrown into the midst of the current, that it may be entirely carried off

Should the cache not be formed in the vicinity of a stream, the earth thus thrown up is carried to a distance, and scattered in such a manner as not to leave the minutest trace. The cave being formed, is well lined with dry grass, bark, sticks, and poles, and occasionally a dried hide. The property intended to be hidden is then laid in, after having been well aired: a hide is spread over it, and dried grass, brush, and stones thrown in, and trampled down until the pit is filled to the neck. The loose soil which had been put aside is then brought, and rammed down firmly, to prevent its caving in, and is frequently sprinkled with water to destroy the scent, lest the wolves and bears should be attracted to the place, and root up the concealed treasure.

When the neck of the cache is nearly level with the surrounding surface, the sod is again fitted in with the utmost exactness, and any bushes, stocks, or stones, that may have originally been about the spot, are restored to their former places. The blankets and other coverings are then removed from the surrounding herbage: all tracks are obliterated: the grass is gently raised by the hand to its natural position, and the minutest chip or straw is scrupulously gleaned up and thrown into the stream. After all is done, the place is abandoned for the night, and, if all be right next morning, is not visited again, until there be a necessity for reopening the cache. Four men are sufficient in this way to conceal the amount of three tons weight of merchandise in the course of two days.

CHAPTER XXIV.

CARSON had passed the autumn and winter with his family, in the society of old companions, amid various incidents amusing to the reader if they were detailed, because so unlike the style of life to which he has been accustomed, the particulars of which we must however leave to his imagination, aiding it by some general description of the customs of the country and locality.

The town of Taos is the second in size in New Mexico (Santa Fé claiming of right to be first), with very little regard to beauty in its construction, the houses being huddled upon narrow streets, except in the immediate vicinity of the *plaza*, on which are located the church and the better class of houses; and where, as in all Mexican towns, the marketing is carried on. It is situated in the center of the valley of Taos, which is about thirty miles long, and fifteen broad, and surrounded by mountains, upon whose tops snow lies during the greater part of the year.

The valley appears to be a plain, but is intersected by many ravines, which flow into the Rio Grande on its western side. There is no timber, but in the mountains it is abundant, and of excellent quality. The population in the whole valley numbers scarcely more than ten thousand, and as their farming operations require but a portion of the soil, the larger part of the land is still wild, and grazed only by horses, cattle, and sheep, which are raised in large numbers.

They are obliged to expend much labor upon their crops, as the climate is too dry to mature them without irrigation; and yet in their community of interest, in a country without fences, they find much satisfaction in rendering kind offices to each other; and social life is more cultivated than in communities whose interests are more separate. The high altitude, and dryness of the atmosphere, render the climate exceedingly healthful, rather severe in winter, but very mild and salubrious in summer, so that disease is scarcely known in the valley.

The dress of the people has changed very much since the population became partially

Americanized, so that often the buckskin pants have given place to cloth, and the blanket to the coat, and the moccasin to the leathern shoe, and the dress of the women has undergone as great a change. They are learning to employ American implements for agriculture, instead of the rude Egyptian yoke fastened to the horns of the oxen; and the plow composed of a single hooked piece of timber, and the ax that more resembles a pick, than the ax of the American woodsman; and the cart, whose wheels are pieces sawed from the butt end of a log, with a hole bored for the axle, whose squeaking can be heard for miles, and which are themselves a sufficient burden without any loading. Their diet is simple, as it is with all Mexicans, consisting of the products of the locality, with game, which is always to be included in a bill of fare such as Carson would furnish; corn, and wheat, and peas, beans, eggs, pumpkins, and apples, pears, peaches, plums, and grapes, constitute the principal products of their culture. Their great source of enjoyment is dancing, and the fandango is so much an institution in a town of the size of Taos, that, during the winter, scarcely a night passes without a dance. This is doubtless familiar to the reader, as the acquisition of California has introduced a knowledge of the customs of its natives to every eastern household.

In the spring of 1845, Carson had decided to commence the business of farming at Taos, and had made the necessary arrangements for building a house, and for stocking and planting, when an express arrived from Colonel Fremont, bringing despatches to remind him of his promise to join a third exploring expedition, in case he should ever undertake another, and to designate the place where he would meet the party Fremont was organizing.

Before parting with Fremont in the previous summer, Fremont had secured the promise from Carson, that he would again be his guide and companion, should he ever undertake another expedition ; but Carson was not expecting its execution at this time, and yet, though it would entail severe loss on him to make a hasty sale of his possessions, and arrange for leaving his family, he felt bound by his promise, as well as by his attachment to Fremont, and at once closing up his business, together with an old friend by the name of Owens, who had become, as it were, a partner with him in his enterprise of farming, they having been old trapping friends, they repaired together to the point designated for joining the exploring party, upon the upper Arkansas, at Bent's Fort, wnere they had last parted from Fremont.

The meeting was mutually satisfactory, and with Fremont were Maxwell, an old and well-tried friend, and a Mr. Walker, who had been in Captain Bonneville's expedition to the Columbia, and in other trapping parties in California and vicinity, so that with other mountain men, whose names are less known, but every man of whom was Carson's friend, Fremont's corps was more efficient for the present service, than it had been in either of the former expeditions.

After some months spent in examining the head-waters of the great rivers which flow to either ocean, the party descended at the beginning of winter to the Great Salt Lake, and in October encamped on its southwestern shore, in view of that undescribed country which at that time had not been penetrated, and which vague and contradictory reports of Indians represented as a desert without grass or water.

Their previous visit to the lake had given it a somewhat familiar aspect, and on leaving it they felt as if about to commence their journey anew. Its eastern shore was frequented by large bands of Indians, but here they had dwindled down to a single family, which was gleaning from some hidden source enough to support life, and drinking the salt water of a little stream near by, no fresh water being at hand. This offered scanty encouragement as to what they might expect on the desert beyond.

At its threshold and immediately before them was a naked plain of smooth clay surface, mostly devoid of vegetation—the hazy weather of the summer hung over it, and in the distance rose scattered, low, black and dry-looking mountains. At what appeared to be fifty miles or more, a higher peak held out some promise of wood and water, and towards this it was resolved to direct their course.

Four men, with a pack animal loaded with water for two days, and accompanied by a naked Indian—who volunteered for a reward to be their guide to a spot where he said there was grass and fine springs—were sent forward to explore in advance for a foothold, and verify the existence of water before the whole party should be launched into the desert. Their way led toward the high peak of the mountain, on which they were to make a smoke signal in the event of finding water. About sunset of the second day, no signal having been seen, Fremont became uneasy at the absence of his men, and set out with the whole party upon their trail, traveling rapidly all the night. Towards morning one of the scouts was met returning.

The Indian had been found to know less than themselves, and had been sent back, but the men had pushed on to the mountains, where they found a running stream, with wood and sufficient grass. The whole party now lay down to rest, and the next day, after a hard march, reached the stream. The distance across the plain was nearly seventy miles, and they called the mountain which had guided them Pilot Peak. This was their first day's march and their first camp in the desert.

A few days afterwards the expedition was divided into two parties—the larger one under the guidance of Walker, a well-known mountaineer and experienced traveler, going around to the foot of the Sierra Nevada by a circuitous route which he had previously traveled, and Fremont, with ten men, Delawares and whites, penetrated directly through the heart of the desert.

Some days after this separation, Fremont's party, led by Carson, while traveling along the foot of a mountain, the arid country covered with dwarf shrubs, discovered a volume of smoke rising from a ravine. Riding cautiously up, they discovered a single Indian on the border of a small creek. He was standing before a little fire, naked as he was born, apparently thinking, and looking at a small earthen pot which was simmering over the fire, filled with the common ground squirrel of the country. Another bunch of squirrels lay near it, and close by were his bow and arrows. He was a well-made, good-looking young man, about twenty-five years of age. Although so taken by surprise that he made no attempt to escape, and evidently greatly alarmed, he received his visitors with forced gaiety, and offered them part of his *pot au feu* and his bunch of squirrels. He was kindly treated and some little presents made him, and the party continued their way.

His bow was handsomely made, and the arrows, of which there were about forty in his quiver, were neatly feathered, and headed with obsidian, worked into spear-shape by patient labor.

After they had separated, Fremont found that his Delawares had taken a fancy to the

Indian's bow and arrows, and carried them off They carried them willingly back, when they were reminded that they had exposed the poor fellow to almost certain starvation by depriving him, in the beginning of winter, of his only means of subsistence, which it would require months to replace.

One day the party had reached one of the lakes lying along the foot of the Sierra Nevada, which was their appointed rendezvous with their friends, and where, at this season, the scattered Indians of the neighborhood were gathering, to fish. Turning a point on the lake shore, a party of Indians, some twelve or fourteen in number, came abruptly in view. They were advancing along in Indian file, one following the other, their heads bent forward, with eyes fixed on the ground. As the two parties met, the Indians did not turn their heads or raise their eyes from the ground, but passed silently along. The whites, habituated to the chances of savage life, and always uncertain whether they should find friends or foes in those they met, fell readily into their humor, and they too passed on their way without word or halt.

It was a strange meeting: two parties of

such different races and different countries, coming abruptly upon each other, with every occasion to excite curiosity and provoke question, pass in a desert without a word of inquiry or single remark on either side, or without any show of hostility.

Walker's party joined Fremont at the appointed rendezvous, at the point where Walker's River discharges itself into the lake, but it was now mid-winter, they were out of provisions—and there was no guide. The heavy snows might be daily expected to block up the passes in the great Sierra, if they had not already fallen, and with all their experience it was considered too hazardous to attempt the passage with the *materiel* of a whole party; it was arranged therefore that Walker should continue with the main party southward along the Sierra, and enter the valley of the San Joaquin by some one of the low passes at its head, where there is rarely or never snow. Fremont undertook, with a few men, to cross directly westward over the Sierra Nevada to Sutter's Fort, with the view of obtaining there the necessary supplies of horses and beef cattle with which to rejoin his party.

After some days' travel, leaving the Mercedes

River, they had entered among the foothills of the mountains, and were journeying through a beautiful country of undulating upland, openly timbered with oaks, principally evergreen, and watered with small streams.

Traveling along, they came suddenly upon broad and deeply-worn trails, which had been freshly traveled by large bands of horses, apparently coming from the settlements on the coast. These and other indications warned them that they were approaching villages of the Horse-Thief Indians, who appeared to have just returned from a successful foray. With the breaking up of the missions, many of the Indians had returned to their tribes in the mountains. Their knowledge of the Spanish language, and familiarity with the ranches and towns, enabled them to pass and repass, at pleasure, between their villages in the Sierra and the ranches on the coast. They very soon availed themselves of these facilities to steal and run off into the mountains bands of horses, and in a short time it became the occupation of all the Indians inhabiting the southern Sierra Nevada, as well as the plains beyond.

Three or four parties would be sent at a time from different villages, and every week was signalized by the carrying-off of hundreds of horses, to be killed and eaten in the interior. Repeated expeditions had been made against them by the Californians, who rarely succeeded in reaching the foot of the mountains, and were invariably defeated when they did.

As soon as this fresh trail had been discovered, four men, two Delawares with Maxwell and Dick Owens, two of Fremont's favorite men, were sent forward upon the trail. The rest of the party had followed along at their usual gait, but Indian signs became so thick, trail after trail joining on, that they started rapidly after the men, fearing for their safety. After a few miles' ride, they reached a spot which had been the recent camping ground of a village, and where abundant grass and good water suggested a halting place for the night, and they immediately set about unpacking their animals and preparing to encamp.

While thus engaged, they heard what seemed to be the barking of many dogs, coming apparently from a village, not far distant; but they had hardly thrown off their saddles when they suddenly became aware that it was the noise of women and children shouting and crying; and this was sufficient notice that the men who had been sent ahead had fallen among unfriendly Indians, so that a fight had already commenced.

It did not need an instant to throw the saddles on again, and leaving four men to guard the camp, Fremont, with the rest, rode off in the direction of the sounds.

They had galloped but half a mile, when crossing a little ridge, they came abruptly in view of several hundred Indians advancing on each side of a knoll, on the top of which were the men, where a cluster of trees and rocks made a good defense. It was evident that they had come suddenly into the midst of the Indian village, and jumping from their horses, with the instinctive skill of old hunters and mountaineers as they were, had got into an admirable place to fight from.

The Indians had nearly surrounded the knoll, and were about getting possession of the horses, as Fremont's party came in view. Their welcome shout as they charged up the hill, was answered by the yell of the Delawares as they dashed down to recover their animals, and the crack of Owens' and Maxwell's rifles. Owens had singled out the foremost Indian who went headlong down the hill, to steal horses no more

Profiting by the first surprise of the Indians, and anxious for the safety of the men who had been left in camp, the whites immediately retreated towards it, checking the Indians with occasional rifle shots, with the range of which it seemed remarkable that they were acquainted.

The whole camp were on guard until daylight. As soon as it was dark, each man crept to his post. They heard the women and children retreating towards the mountains, but nothing disturbed the quiet of the camp, except when one of the Delawares shot at a wolf as it jumped over a log, and which he mistook for an Indian. As soon as it grew light they took to the most open ground, and retreated into the plain.

CHAPTER XXV.

THE record of Fremont and Carson's journey through this region of country, already so thoroughly explored at such great hazard, and accompanied with such unheard-of sufferings, would be but a repetition of what has already been written, for they were again driven to mule meat, or whatever else chance or Providence might throw in their way, to sustain life. In every need—in every peril—in every quarter where coolness, sagacity, and skill were most required, Carson was ever first, and his conduct throughout cemented, if possible, more firmly the friendship between him and his young commander.

They reached, at last, Sutter's Fort, where they were received with the hospitality which has made Mr. Sutter's name proverbial; and leaving his party to recruit there, Fremont pushed on towards Monterey, to make known to the authorities there the condition of his party, and obtained permission to recruit and procure the supplies necessary for the prosecution of his exploration.

Journeying in the security of this permission, he was suddenly arrested in his march, near Monterey, by an officer at the head of a body of cavalry, who bore him a violent message from the commanding officer in California—Gen. Castro—commanding him to retire instantly from the country.

There was now no alternative but to put himself on the defensive, as he had come to the country for an entirely peaceable purpose, and it was not in the blood of Americans to submit to dictation. The direction of travel was therefore changed; a strong point was selected and fortified as thoroughly as could be with the means at their command, which work was hardly completed before General Castro, at the head of several hundred men, arrived and established his camp within a few hundred yards and in sight of the exploring party, evidently under the mistaken idea that he could intimidate them by his numbers.

Though the Americans were but forty in number, every man had already seen service, and the half score of old traders and trappers, who had been leaders in many an Indian fight, made the party, small as it was, quite equal to that of the tenfold greater number of the Mexicans; for the men, equally with their leader, were determined to maintain their rights, and, if need be, to sacrifice their lives in defense of the cause of American citizens in Mexico; for in the three days during which they lay there encamped, expresses came in from the American citizens in Monterey, warning them of their danger, and announcing, too, the probability of a war with Mexico, and urging the propriety that every American should unite in a common defense against the Mexican authorities.

At the end of three days the council which Fremont now called, agreed with him, that the Mexican General had no intention of attacking them, and that it was the more prudent course to break up camp, push on to the Sacramento River, and endeavor at Lawson's trading post to obtain the needed outfit for their return homeward through Oregon, as further exploration in southern California seemed out of the question; and because, as an officer in the United States service, Fremont felt he could not commence, or willingly court, hostility with the Mexican authorities—besides, all the American residents in the country were equally in peril; and if the event of war pressed upon them, preparation was needed, and should be made at once.

In council Fremont found Carson ready for such, as for every emergency; and, around the camp fires, where the subject was discussed, every man was ready for the affray; and while willing to retire and wait the command of the leader evinced no disposition to avoid it.

The party remained ten days at Lawson's post, when information was brought that the Indians were in arms at the instigation of the Mexicans, as it was supposed, and were advancing to destroy the post, and any other American settlement; and it was soon rumored that a thousand warriors were collected, and on their way to aid in this purpose. The time had now come for action, and, with five men from the post, Captain Fremont and his command, with Carson for his Lieutenant, by choice of the party, as well as of its leader, took up their march against the savages, in aid of their countrymen.

They had no difficulty in finding the Indian war-party, and immediately made the attack, which was responded to with vigor by the Indians, and contested bravely; but, of course, with inability to conquer. The red men were defeated with terrible slaughter, and learned here the lesson not forgotten for many years, that it was useless to measure their strength with white men.

Carson was, of course, as was his invariable custom, in the thickest of the fight, and when it was over, and the Indians had retired, cowed and defeated, ventured the opinion that they had received a lesson which would not be required to be repeated in many years.

This victory won, and present danger from these Indians thus avoided, the party returned to Lawson's post, where, having completed their outfit, they turned their backs on Mexican possessions, and started northward, Fremont looking to Oregon as the field of his future operations, intending to explore a new route to the Wah-lah-math settlements.

While on that journey, Carson being as ever his guide, companion, and friend, the party was suddenly surprised by the appearance of two white men, who, as all knew from experience, must have incurred the greatest perils and hazards to reach that spot.

They proved to be two of Mr. Fremont's old *voyageurs*, and quickly told their story. They were part of a guard of six men conducting a United States officer, who was on his trail with despatches from Washington, and whom they had left two days back, while they came on to give notice of his approach, and to ask that assistance might be sent him. They themselves had only escaped the Indians by the swiftness of their horses. It was a case in which there was no time to be lost, nor a mistake made. Mr. Fremont determined to go himself; and taking ten picked men, Carson of course accompanying him, he rode down the western shore of the lake on the morning of the 9th, (the direction the officer was to come,) and made a journey of sixty miles without a halt. But to meet men, and not to miss them, was the difficult point in this trackless region. It was not the case of a high-road, where all travelers must meet in passing each other: at intervals there were places—defiles, or camping grounds— where both parties might pass; and watching for these, he came to one in the afternoon, and decided that, if the party was not killed, it must be there that night. He halted and encamped; and, as the sun was going down, had the inexpressible satisfaction to see the four men approaching. The officer proved to be

Lieutenant Gillespie, of the United States Marines, who had been despatched from Washington the November previous, to make his way by Vera Cruz, the City of Mexico, and Mazatlan, to Monterey, in Upper California, deliver despatches to the United States consul there; and then find Mr. Fremont, wherever he should be.

Carson, in a letter to the Washington Union in June, 1847, thus describes the interview, and the events consequent upon it:

"Mr. Gillespie had brought the Colonel letters from home—the first he had had since leaving the States the year before—and he was up, and kept a large fire burning until after midnight; the rest of us were tired out, and all went to sleep. This was the only night in all our travels, except the one night on the island in the Salt Lake, that we failed to keep guard; and as the men were so tired, and we expected no attack now that we had sixteen in the party, the Colonel didn't like to ask it of them, but sat up late himself. Owens and I were sleeping together, and we were waked at the same time by the licks of the ax that killed our men. At first, I didn't know it was that; but I called to Basil, who was on that side —'What'— the matter there?—What's that fuss about?'—he never answered, for he was dead then, poor fellow, and he never knew what killed him—his head had been cut in, in his sleep; the other groaned a little as he died. The Delawares (we had four with us) were sleeping at that fire, and they sprang up as the Tlamaths charged them. One of them caught up a gun, which was unloaded; but, although he could do no execution, he kept them at bay, fighting like a soldier, and didn't give up until he was shot full of arrows— three entering his heart; he died bravely. As soon as I had called out, I saw it was Indians in the camp, and I and Owens together cried out "Indians." There were no orders given; things went on too fast, and the Colonel had men with him that didn't need to be told their duty. The Colonel and I, Maxwell, Owens, Godey, and Stepp, jumped together, we six, and ran to the assistance of our Delawares. I don't know who fired and who didn't; but I think it was Stepp's shot that killed the Tlamath chief; for it was at the crack of Stepp's gun that he fell. He had an English half-ax slung to his wrist by a cord, and there were forty arrows left in his quiver—the most beautiful and warlike arrows I ever saw. He must have been the bravest man among them, from the way he was armed, and judging by his cap. When the Tlamaths saw him fall, they ran; but we lay, every man with his rifle cocked until daylight, expecting another attack.

"In the morning we found by the tracks that from fifteen to twenty of the Tlamaths had attacked us. They had killed three of our men, and wounded one of the Delawares, who scalped the chief, whom we left where he fell. Our dead men were carried on mules; but, after going about ten miles, we found it impossible to get them any farther through the thick timber, and finding a secret place, we buried them under logs and chunks, having no way to dig a grave. It was only a few days before this fight that some of these same Indians had come into our camp; and, although we had only meat for two days, and felt sure that we should have to eat mules for ten or fifteen days to come, the Colonel divided with them, and even had a mule unpacked to give them some tobacco and knives."

CHAPTER XXVI.

Those who have not been in similar dangers cannot properly appreciate the feelings of the survivors, as they watched with their dead and performed for them the last sad rites. Fremont had lost Lajeunesse, whom they all loved, and the other two, Crane and the Delaware Indian, were not less brave than he. The Indians had watched for Lieutenant Gillespie, but in Fremont's coming up while three were taken, more were saved, and the benefit to the country, and perhaps the safety to Fremont's whole force was secured by the receipt of the despatches, and this early rencontre. None had apprehended danger that night, being, as they erroneously supposed, far removed from the Tlamath country, and equally far from the point where they already had encountered and defeated the red men. The Indians never again found Fremont's party off guard, for the events of this night proved a serious and melancholy, as well as a sufficient lesson. That they cherished revenge, is not to be wondered at, nor that they vowed to seek it at the earliest opportunity, as it was now known that war had been declared with Mexico, for such was the tenor of Lieutenant Gillespie's information. Fremont determined to return to California, and choosing to give his men a chance for revenge before doing so, he traveled around Tlamath Lake, and, camping at a spot nearly opposite where his three men had been killed, the next morning sent Carson on in advance, with ten chosen men, and with instructions that, if he discovered a large Indian village, without being seen himself, he should send back word, and that he would hasten on with the rest of the party and give them battle; but if this could not be done, to attack the village himself, if he thought the chances were equal.

Of course Carson and his men were parties to this advice, choosing the situation of danger because only in that way could they revenge the death of their comrades.

They were not long in finding a trail, which they followed to a village of fifty lodges, in each of which were probably three warriors. The village was in commotion, which indicated that they had discovered Carson and his party;

so that no time could be lost, and Carson and his comrades at once determined to take advantage of the confusion in which the Indian camp seemed to be, by making a sudden charge.

The Indians had their families to defend, and were brave in proportion as that motive is an incentive to activity, therefore the attack of the white men was received and met with desperation. But a panic of fear seized them, owing to the suddenness of the attack, and they fled, leaving behind them all their possessions, while the victors pursued and shot them down without mercy, and when the victory was declared complete by their leader Carson, they returned to the richly-stored village. In all their travels and adventures, they had never seen an Indian village in which the lodges were more tasteful in their workmanship and their decorations, or which were better supplied with utensils of convenience. The wigwams were woven of the broad leaves of a kind of flag which was highly combustible. Carson therefore ordered that they should be burned, having first visited them to see that their contents were so arranged as to be consumed in the conflagration. The work was completed in a few moments, and Fremont, seeing the smoke, knew that Carson was engaged with the Indians, and hastened forward to render him any needed assistance. But he arrived only to hear the report of his lieutenant, and to have the gloom of the whole party dispelled by the news of the victory accomplished; and to move on a little for an encampment, and a talk in regard to their future operations.

The next day all started for the valley of the Sacramento, and were four days out from their camp when they came to a point on the river where it passes through a deep cañon, through which the trail would take them, but Carson advised to avoid this gorge, and they were wise in doing so, as Tlamath Indians were concealed there, intending to cut off the party of white men. Disappointed that they had lost their prey, the Indians came out from this ambush, and were immediately dispersed by Carson and Godey, and a few others, who made a charge upon them. But one old Indian, inspired probably by revenge for some friend lost, stood his ground, and with several arrows in his mouth waited the attack he courted. Carson and Godey advanced, and when within shooting distance, were obliged to dodge rapidly to avoid the arrows leveled at them. The Indian was behind a tree, and only by cautiously advancing while dodging the death he was sending from his bow, did Carson gain a position where he was able to aim a bullet at his heart. The beautiful bow and still unexhausted quiver that Carson took from this Indian, he presented to Lieutenant Gillespie on his return to camp.

They were in the locality where game was scarce, not being able to find any, the whole party went supperless that night and breakfastless next morning, but the next day they found some game, and came, after severe traveling for some days longer, safely in to Peter Lawson's Fort, where they rested and hunted a week, and then moved lower down on the Sacramento, and again camped. But his men were restless from inactivity, and Fremont decided it was no longer wise to wait for positive instructions, as the war was probably commenced; he therefore sent a party of his force to take the little town and fort at Sonoma, which had but a weak garrison. They captured General Vallejos here with two captains and several cannon, and a quantity of arms. The whole force united at Sonoma, and learning that the Mexicans and Americans in the south were engaged in open hostility, Fremont was preparing to join them, calling in all the Americans in the vicinity to come to his command, when a large Mexican force, despatched by General Castro from San Francisco, with orders to drive the Americans out of the country, came into the vicinity, and took prisoners and killed two men, whom Fremont had sent out as messengers to the American settlers, to inform them that Sonoma was taken, and that they could fly thither for safety.

The captain of this party of Mexicans, hearing that Fremont and his forces were anxious to attack him, lost all courage and fled, to be pursued by the party of explorers, who followed them closely for six days, and captured many horses which they had abandoned in their fright. But finding they could not overtake them, Fremont returned to Sonoma, and the party of Mexicans continued their march to Los Angeles, where General Castro joined them.

Around Fremont's party, the American citizens now rallied in great numbers—nearly all who were in the country—knowing that their time to aid in its emancipation had arrived. Fremont left a strong garrison at Sonoma, and went to Sutter's Fort, where he left his prisoners General Vallejos and the two captains, and an American. a brother-in-law of General Vallejos, and having put the fort under military rules, with all his mountain men, started to take possession of Monterey. But he had been anticipated in this work by Commodore Sloat, who was in port with the American squadron, and who left soon after Fremont's arrival, Commodore Stockton assuming the command.

While at Sonoma, Fremont and his mountain men, with the American settlers, had declared the Independence of California, and assumed the Bear Flag, which he gallantly tendered to Commodore Sloat, and the flag of the United States was hoisted over his camp.

CHAPTER XXVII.

WITH Carson as his constant adviser, as he was now his acknowledged friend, Fremont here obtained the use of the ship Cyanne, to convey himself and his command to San Diego, where they hoped to be able to obtain animals, and march upon the Mexicans under General Castro, who was then at Los Angeles, leaving their own for the use of Commodore Stockton and his marines, who were to meet them at that place.

With the Americans who joined him at San Diego, all of them pioneers of the true stamp, inured to hardships, hard fare, and Indian fights, Fremont's command numbered one hundred and fifty men, who started for Los Angeles, with perfect confidence in their own success, though the force of the enemy was seven or eight hundred.

Fremont camped a league from this beautiful town, to await the arrival of the Commodore who soon joined him. with " as fine a body of men as I ever looked upon," to quote Carson's own words, and the forces thus united marched at once upon Los Angeles, which they found deserted, as General Castro dared not risk a battle with such men as he knew Fremont commanded.

After this, Fremont was appointed Governor of California by Commodore Stockton, and returned to Monterey and the northern portion of the country, while the Commodore went to San Diego, as that was a better port than San Pedro, the port of Los Angeles; and General Castro returned to the possession of Los Angeles.

Meantime, Carson, with a force of fifteen men, was despatched to make the overland journey to Washington, as the bearer of important despatches. He was instructed to make the journey in sixty days if possible, which he felt sure of being able to accomplish, though no one knew, better than he did, the difficulties he might expect to encounter.

When two days out from the copper mines of New Mexico, he came suddenly upon a village of Apache Indians, which his quick wit enabled him to elude. He rode forward in his path, as if unmindful of their presence, and halted in a wood a few yards from the village, which seemed to disconcert the inhabitants, unused to being approached with so much boldness, as they had never been treated in that manner by the Mexicans. He here demanded a parley, which was granted, and he told them that his party were simply travelers on the road to New Mexico, and that they had come to their village for an exchange of animals, as theirs were nearly exhausted.

The Indians were satisfied with his explanation; and Carson, choosing as his camping-ground a suitable spot for defense, traded with the Apaches to advantage, and at an early hour on the following morning resumed his journey, glad to be thus easily rid of such treacherous, thieving rascals. A few more days of travel brought him to the Mexican settlements, and near to his own home and family. The party had been, for some time, short of provisions, as their haste in traveling did not allow them to stop to hunt, and on the route—desert much of the way—there had been little game; and now, with only a little corn which they ate parched, they were glad of relief, which Carson readily obtained from friends at the first ranche he entered; for though the country was at war with the United States, Carson was a Mexican as much as an American, having chosen their country for his home, and taken a wife from their people. He was pursuing his course towards Taos, when, across a broad prairie, he espied a speck moving towards him, which his eagle eye soon discerned could not belong to the country. As it neared him, and its form became visible, hastening on, he met an expedition sent out by the United States Government to operate in California, under the command of General Kearney, to which officer he lost no time in presenting himself, and narrated to him his errand, and the state of affairs in California, with the most graphic fidelity. Kearney was extremely glad to meet him, and after detaining him as long as Carson thought it wise to remain, proposed to Carson to return with him, while he should send the despatches to Washington by Mr. Fitzpatrick—with whom Carson had a familiar acquaintance; and knowing how almost invaluable his services would be to General Kearney, Carson gave the ready answer, "As the General pleases," trusting entirely to his fidelity in the matter, and as the exchange was a self-denial to him, he had no occasion to weigh the motives that might influence a man like General Kearney in the affair of the despatches, or the good that his presence with them might be to himself when he should arrive in Washington, but while he would have been glad to have met his family, he cared for the honor of having done his duty.

CHAPTER XXVIII.

On the 18th of October, General Kearney took up his march from his camp upon the Rio Grande, having Christopher Carson for his guide, with instructions to lead the party by the most direct route to California: and so ably did Carson fulfil this official duty, so unexpectedly imposed upon him, that, with their animals in good condition still, they camped within the limit of California on the evening of the third of December, and the next morning advanced towards San Diego.

But the Mexicans were not unapprised of the approach of American troops, and spies sent out by General Castro, to meet Kearney's force, were surprised and brought into camp by a scout which Carson attended. Compelled to give information, they said that the Mexican forces under its general were planning an attack upon the Americans before they could join their California allies. Carson, with the anderstanding he had of General Kearney, and his knowledge of guerilla warfare, would have advised another route, to evade the Mexican troops and avoid a battle, until the weary and newly arrived soldiery had had some rest, and the assistance and advice of those who knew the last movements of the Mexicans, could make a battle more effectual with less of risk than now; but General Kearney was impatient for an encounter with the stupid Mexicans, as he deemed them, and only learned by experience that the Californians were superior to those he had known in other of the Mexican States, both in courage and natural tact, and in their military order and discipline, as the story will fully show.

He kept on his course until he approached within fifteen miles of the Mexican camp, where he halted, and despatched a party to reconnoiter. They reported on their return, that the enemy were strongly fortified in an Indian village; but in making the observation the scout had been discovered and pursued back to camp.

General Kearney determined to make an immediate attack, and commenced his march at one o'clock in the morning, with no rest that night for his animals or for his men; and weary and hungry before day, when within a mile of Castro's camp the advance guard of the Americans came upon the advance guard of the Mexicans, which had been stationed to prevent a surprise.

This Mexican guard slept in their dress, ready at a five minutes' warning to mount in their saddles, which were their pillows, while their horses were tied to feed close around them. The sound of the trumpet commanded first a rapid trot, then a gallop, and the fifteen Americans under Captain Johnson with Kit Carson, of course, for his next officer, had a brisk fight with this Mexican outpost, but failed to stampede their animals, as each Mexican mounted his own horse immediately and the guard drew back into camp. Captain Johnson and Carson were now joined by Captain Moore with twenty five Americans, a force that had united with Kearney's since he came into California, when Moore ordered an attack upon the center of the Mexican force, in order to divide it, and cause confusion in the Mexican ranks.

The command of forty men were within a hundred yards of the enemy, and Carson among the foremost, when his horse suddenly fell and threw its rider, who was not seriously injured; but the stock of his gun was shivered to splinters, and his position one of exceeding danger, as the whole body of dragoons went galloping over him. When he could arise from the ground, he saw a dead horseman lying near, whom he relieved of gun and cartridge box, and again mounting his horse, upon whose bridle he had managed to retain his hold, he was speedily in the thickest of the fight, where the contest was becoming desperate.

Captain Johnson and several of the soldiers in the advance had already been killed, and probably only the fall of his horse had saved Carson's life, but he was now able to assist Moore and his men to dislodge the Mexicans, and oblige them to retreat. The Americans pursued them, but as there were only forty in the whole of General Kearney's command who were mounted on horses, and the mules which were ridden by the rest had become at once unmanageable when the firing commenced, their success was not complete. The horses they had were wild, having been captured by Captain Davidson and Kit Carson since their arrival in California, from a party of Mexicans bound for Sonora, so that even Moore's party had become scattered in the chase, and the pursuit accomplished very little.

The Mexicans immediately discovered the condition of the Americans, and turning back, recommenced the fight, which had been nearly a bloodless victory until now, but soon became for the Americans a terrible slaughter. Every moment some dragoon yielded his life to the bullet or the deadly blow of an exasperated Mexican, and of the forty dragoons on horses thirty were either killed or severely wounded. Captain Moore, whom Carson calls, "as brave a man as ever drew the breath of life," was already among the killed. As fast as the American soldiers could come up, they joined the battle, but the Mexicans fought with a bravery unsurpassed, and seemed to carry all before them.

General Kearney now drew his sword, and placed himself at the head of his remaining forces, and though severely wounded, attempted to again force the Mexicans to retreat, while Lieutenant Davidson came up with two mountain howitzers; but before he could unlimber them for use, the men who were working them were shot down, and the lasso, thrown with unerring aim, had captured the horses attached to one of them, and the gun was taken to the ranks of the enemy, who, for some reason could not make it go off, or the American howitzer, at the distance of three hundred yards, would have done execution against those who had brought it thousands of miles to this point, to have it turned against them; though Lieutenant Davidson had nearly lost his life in the attempt to save it, but to no purpose.

The Americans were now obliged to take refuge at a point of rocks that offered, near where they had been defeated, for they had but two officers besides Carson, who were not either killed or wounded; and here they waited for the Mexicans, but they did not again venture an attack.

The fighting had continued throughout the entire day; both sides were weary and spent, and night closed over this scene of battle, without any positive result to either party. General Kearney must now attend to the wounded, and all night the camp was occupied in the sad work of burying its dead, and alleviating the agony of the sufferers; while, at the same time, a close watch was kept for the enemy, who were constantly receiving reinforcements, of Indians as well as Mexicans, from the country around. A council of war was held, which at once decided it was best to advance toward San Diego in the morning, with the hope of soon receiving additions to their forces. General Kearney had despatched three men to San Diego, with messages to Commodore Stockton, and before the battle commenced, they had come back within sight of their comrades, when they were taken prisoners by the enemy; and whether they had succeeded in getting through to San Diego, General Kearney did not know. Early in the morning, the command was again upon its way, with the following order of march: Carson, with twenty-five still able-bodied men, formed the advance, and the remainder, a much crippled band of soldiers, followed in the trail that he had made. Their march was continued all the morning, in the constant expectation of an attack from the Mexicans, who were also moving on, sometimes out of sight in the valleys, and sometimes seen from the neighboring hills. When the first opportunity occurred, General Kearney demanded a parley, and arranged to exchange a lieutenant, whose horse had been shot from under him during the battle and who had consequently fallen into the hands of the Americans, for one of the express messengers the Mexicans were detaining ; but it availed nothing, for the expressman stated that, finding it impossible to reach San Diego, he and his companions had returned, when they were captured by the Mexicans.

The Mexicans had been maneuvering all day, and toward evening, as the Americans were about going into camp by a stream of water, came down upon them in two divisions, making a vigorous charge. The Americans were obliged to retire before such vastly superior numbers, and marched in order to a hill a little distance off, where they halted to give the Mexicans battle ; but the latter, seeing the advantage of the position, drew off to a neighboring height, where they commenced and continued a deadly cannonade upon the Americans. A party of Americans was sent to dislodge them, which they accomplished, and the whole force of the Americans went over to occupy that position, as they were compelled to make a resting place somewhere, because it was no longer possible for them to continue their march, with the Mexican force ready at any time to fall upon them. Upon this hill there was barely water enough for the men, and to take the horses to the stream could not be thought of, for the Mexicans would surely capture them; nor had they any food left, except as they killed and ate their mules.

The condition of the party had become extremely desperate, and the war council that was called discussed a variety of measures, equally desperate with their condition, for immediate relief, until, when the rest had made their propositions, Carson again showed himself " the right man in the right place," and when all besides were hopeless, was the salvation of his party. He rose in the council and said:

" Our case *is* a desperate one, but there is yet hope. If we stay here, we are all dead men; our animals cannot last long, and the soldiers and marines at San Diego do not know of our coming. But if they receive information of our position, they would hasten to our rescue. There is no use in thinking why or how we are here, but only of our present and speedy escape. I will attempt to go through the Mexican lines, and will then go to San Diego, and send relief from Commodore Stockton."

Lieutenant Beale, of the United States Navy, at once seconded Carson, and volunteered to accompany him.

Lieutenant Beale is now widely known for his valuable services to the country, and, as an explorer, he has few equals in the world.

The writer is informed that he is now deeply interested in a wagon road across the country by the route he had just crossed, at the time of which we write. His life has been full of strange adventures, since he left the service of the seas.

General Kearney immediately accepted the proposal of Carson and Lieutenant Beale, as his only hope, and they started at once, as soon as the cover of darkness was hung around them. Their mission was to be one of success or of death to themselves and the whole force. Carson was familiar with the custom of the Mexicans, as well as the Indians, of putting their ear to the ground to detect any sound, and knew, therefore, the necessity of avoiding the slightest noise. As this was not possible, wearing their shoes, they removed them, and putting them under their belts, crept on over the bushes and rocks, with the greatest caution and silence.

They discovered that the Mexicans had three rows of sentinels, whose beats extended past each other, embracing the hill where Kearney and his command were held in siege. They were, doubtless, satisfied that they could not be eluded. But our messengers crept on, often so near a sentinel as to see his figure and equipment in the darkness; and once, when within a few yards of them, one of the sentinels had dismounted and lighted his cigarette with his flint and steel. Kit Carson seeing this, as he lay flat on the ground, had put his foot back and touched Lieutenant Beale, a signal to be still as he was doing. The minutes the Mexican was occupied in this way seemed hours to our heroes, who expected they were discovered; and Carson affirms that they were so still he could hear Lieutenant Beale's heart pulsate, and in the agony of the time he lived a year. But the Mexican finally mounted his horse, and rode off in a contrary direction, as if he were guided by Providence, to give safety to these courageous adventurers. For full two miles Kit Carson and Lieutenant Beale thus worked their way along, upon their hands and knees, turning their eyes in every direction to detect anything which might lead to their discovery, and having passed the last sentinel, and left the lines sufficiently behind them, they felt an immeasurable relief in once more gaining their feet

But their shoes were gone, and in the excitement of the journey, neither of them had thought of their shoes since they first put them in their belts; but they could speak again, and congratulate each other that the imminent danger was past, and thank heaven that they had been aided thus far. But there were still abundant difficulties, as their path was rough with bushes, from the necessity of avoiding the well-trodden trail lest they be detected; and the prickly pear covered the ground, and its thorns penetrated their feet at every step; and their road was lengthened by going around out of the direct path, though the latter would have shortened their journey many a weary mile. All the day following they pursued their journey, and on still, without cessation, into the night following, for they could not stop until assured that relief was to be furnished to their anxious and perilous conditioned fellow-soldiers.

Carson had pursued so straight a course, and aimed so correctly for his mark, that they entered the town by the most direct passage, and answering "friends" to the challenge of the sentinel, it was known from whence they came, and they were at once conducted to Commo dore Stockton, to whom they related the errand on which they had come, and the further particulars we have described.

Commodore Stockton immediately detailed a force of nearly two hundred men, and with his usual promptness, ordered them to seek their besieged countrymen by forced marches.

They took with them a piece of ordnance, which the men were obliged to draw themselves, as there were in readiness no animals to be had. Carson did not return with them, as his feet were in a terrible condition, and he needed to rest or he might lose them, but he described the position of General Kearney so accurately, that the party to relieve him would find him with no difficulty; and yet, if the Commodore had expressed the wish, he would have undertaken to conduct the relief party upon its march.

Lieutenant Beale was partially deranged for several days, from the effects of this severe service, and was sent on board the frigate lying in port for medical attendance; but he did not fully recover his former physical health for more than two years; but he never spoke regretfully of an undertaking, which was not excelled by any feat performed in the Mexican war.

The reinforcement reached General Kearney without a collision with the Mexicans, and very soon all marched to San Diego, where the wounded soldiers received medical attendance.

We have spoken of the superiority of character of the California Mexicans over that of the inhabitants of the other Mexican States. The officials appointed at the Mexican capital for this State were treated deferentially or cavalierly, as they consulted or disregarded the wishes of the people, and often it happened that a Governor-General of California was put on board a ship at Monterey, and directed to betake himself back to those who sent him.

California was so remote from the headquarters of the general government, that these things were done with impunity, for it would have been difficult to send a force into the State that could subdue it, with its scattered population, and if laws obnoxious to them were enacted, and they violated them, or expelled an official who proposed their enforcement, it was quietly overlooked. Managing their own affairs in this way, a spirit of independence and bold daring had been cultivated, especially since the time when our story of California life commenced in Carson's first visit to that State, nor had the intercourse with Americans hitherto lessened these feelings, for the California Mexicans admired the Americans, as they called them, and cultivated good fellowship with them generally; so that we see when the Bear Flag and Independence of the State became the order under Fremont and his party, many of its leading citizens came at once into the arrangement, or were parties in it at the first.

Had the conquest and government of the country been conducted wholly by Fremont, it would have exhibited very little expenditure of life, for conciliation and the cultivation of kindly feeling was the policy he pursued; indeed, with Carson as prime counselor, whose wife at home in Taos owned kindred with this people as one of the same race, how could it have been otherwise! though as Americans and citizens of the United States, in whose employ they acted, first allegiance was ever cheerfully accorded to their country, by Carson equally with Fremont, as the history of California most fully proves.

The United States forces at San Diego were not in condition to again take the field, until a number of weeks had elapsed, when a command of six hundred had been organized for the purpose of again capturing Los Angeles, where the Mexican forces were concentrated, and General Kearney and Commodore Stockton were united in conducting it, and in two days arrived within fifteen miles of the town, near where the Mexican army, to the number of seven hundred, had established themselves strongly upon a hill beside their camp, and between whom and the Americans flowed a stream of water.

General Kearney ordered two pieces of artillery planted where they would rake the position of the Mexicans, which soon forced them to break up their camp, when General Kearney and Commodore Stockton immediately marched into the town, but only to find it destitute of any military control, as the Mexican army had gone northward to meet Colonel Fremont who had left Monterey with a force of four hundred Americans, to come to Los Angeles.

The Mexicans found Colonel Fremont, and laid down their arms to him, probably preferring to give him the honor of the victory rather than General Kearney, though if this was or was not the motive, history now sayeth not. Colonel Fremont continued his march and came to Los Angeles, and as the fighting for the present certainly was over, he and his men rested here for the winter, where Carson, who had been rendering all the aid in his power to General Kearney, now gladly joined his old commander.

The position of the American forces, had the camps been harmonious, was as comfortable and conducive to happiness during the winter as it was possible for it to be, and the Mexican citizens of Los Angeles had been so conciliated, the time might have passed pleasantly. But, as we have intimated, General Kearney had a general contempt for the Mexicans, and his position in the camp forbade those pleasant civilities which had commenced in San Diego before his arrival, and would have been prosecuted in Los Angeles, to the advantage of all concerned; for, as many of the men in Fremont's camp were old residents of the country, and known and respected by the Mexican citizens, with whom some of them had contracted intimate social relations, it is not wonderful that the Mexican officers and soldiers chose to lay down their arms to him and his command. Fremont had beside, at the instigation of Carson as well as of his own inclination, taken every reasonable opportunity to gratify their love of social life, by joining in their assemblies as opportunity offered; and for this, as well as his magnanimous courage, we can appreciate their choice in giving him the palm of victory.

CHAPTER XXIX.

EVENTS transpire rapidly when a country is in a state of revolution. Early in March of '46 the little party of explorers received the "first hostile message" from General Castro—the *Commandant* General of California—which, though really a declaration of war, upon a party sent out by the United States Government on a purely scientific expedition, had been received and acted upon by Fremont with moderation, and actual war had not been declared until July, when Sonoma was taken, and the flag of independence hoisted on the fourth of that month, and Fremont elected Governor of California.

While hearing indefinitely of these events, Commodore Sloat, who, with the vessels belonging to his command, was lying at Monterey, had hoisted the flag of the United States over that city, anticipating any command to do so on the part of his government, and anticipating also the action of the com mander of the British ship of war, sent for a similar purpose, which arrived at Monterey on the 19th of July, under the command of Sir George Seymour; one of whose officers, in a book published by him after his return to England, describes the entrance of Fremont and his party into Monterey as follows:

"During our stay in Monterey," says Mr. Walpole, "Captain Fremont and his party arrived. They naturally excited curiosity. Here were true trappers, the class that produced the heroes of Fenimore Cooper's best works. These men had passed years in the wilds, living upon their own resources; they were a curious set. A vast cloud of dust appeared first, and thence in long file emerged this wildest wild party. Fremont rode ahead, a spare, active-looking man, with such an eye! He was dressed in a blouse and leggings, and wore a felt hat. After him came five Delaware Indians, who were his body-guard, and had been with him through all his wanderings; they had charge of two baggage horses. The rest, many of them blacker than the Indians, rode two and two, the rifle held by one hand across the pommel of the saddle. Thirty-nine of them are his regular men, the rest are loafers picked up lately; his original men are principally backwoodsmen, from the State of Tennessee and the banks of the upper waters of the Missouri. He has one or two with him who enjoy a high reputation in the prairies. Kit Carson is as well known there as 'the Duke' is in Europe. The dress of these men was principally a long loose coat of deer skin, tied with thongs in front; trowsers of the same, of their own manufacture, which, when wet through, they take off, scrape well inside with a knife, and put on as soon as dry; the saddles were of various fashions, though these and a large drove of horses, and a brass field-gun, were things they had picked up about California. They are allowed no liquor, tea and sugar only; this, no doubt, has much to do with their good conduct; and the discipline, too, is very strict. They were marched up to an open space on the hills near the town, under some large fires, and there took up their quarters, in messes of six or seven, in the open air. The Indians lay beside their leader. One man, a doctor, six feet six high, was an odd-looking fellow. May I never come under his hands!"

Commodore Stockton had arrived the same day with Fremont and Carson and their com mand, and under him Fremont had been appointed General in Chief of the California forces, with Carson for his first Lieutenant; Stockton assuming the civil office of Governor of the country. This had been deemed a measure of necessity, from the fact that the California Mexicans had not yet learned, from the Mexican authorities, the actual declaration of war between the United States and Mexico; and therefore looked upon the operations of the Americans as the acts of adventurers for their own aggrandizement; and yet, with all the intensity of feeling such ideas aroused, Fremont and Carson had won their admiration and their hearts, by the rapidity of their movements, their sudden and effective blows, and the effort by despatch to avoid all cruelty and bloodshed as far as possible.

In this way had San Diego, San Pedro, Los Angeles, Santa Barbara, and the whole country, as the Mexican authorities declared, come into the possession of Commodore Stockton and General Fremont, as a conquered territory, taken in behalf of the United States; and the whole work been completed in about sixty days from the time the first blow was struck; and when all was accomplished, and the conquest complete, Carson started upon his errand to communicate the intelligence to the general government at Washington; with the knowledge that all the leading citizens of California, native as well as the American settlers, were friendly to Fremont, and on his account to Commodore Stockton.

During the three months of Carson's absence, events had transpired that made it necessary to do this work over again, resulting in a measure from the indiscretions of American officers, which induced insurrection on the part of the Mexicans. The arrival of General Kearney with United States troops still further excited them, and produced results which were everything but pleasant to Fremont and Commodore Stockton, the details of which we forbear to give, simply saying that Carson's regard for Fremont showed itself by his return to his service, and doing all that he could to forward his interests, and in his often attending him in his excursions. Fremont's command was an independent battalion; and concerning the last and final contest, General Kearney thus wrote to the War Department:

"This morning, Lieutenant-Colonel Fremont, of the regiment of mounted riflemen, reached here with four hundred volunteers from the Sacramento; the enemy capitulated with him yesterday, near San Fernando, agreeing to lay down their arms; and we have now the prospect of having peace and quietness in this country, which I hope may not be interrupted again."

It was during Carson's absence, en route for Washington, that Fremont accomplished the most extraordinary feat of physical energy and endurance ever recorded. We find it in the "National Intelligencer," of November 22, 1847, and quote it entire, as illustrating not only the physical powers of human endurance produced by practise and culture, but the wonderful sagacity and enduring qualities of the California horses:

"THE EXTRAORDINARY RIDE OF LIEUT.-COL. FREMONT, HIS FRIEND DON JESUS PICO, AND HIS SERVANT, JACOB DODSON, FROM LOS ANGELES TO MONTEREY AND BACK IN MARCH, 1847.

"This extraordinary ride of 800 miles in eight days, including all stoppages and near two days' detention—a whole day and a night at Monterey, and nearly two half-days at San Luis

Obispo—having been brought into evidence before the Army Court Martial now in session in this city, and great desire being expressed by some friends to know how the ride was made, I herewith send you the particulars, that you may publish them, if you please, in the National Intelligencer, as an incident connected with the times and affairs under review in the trial, of which you give so full a report. The circumstances were first got from Jacob, afterwards revised by Colonel Fremont, and I drew them up from his statement.

"The publication will show, besides the horsemanship of the riders, the power of the California horse, especially as one of the horses was subjected, in the course of the ride, to an extraordinary trial, in order to exhibit the capacity of his race. Of course this statement will make no allusion to the objects of the journey, but be confined strictly to its performance.

"It was at daybreak on the morning of the 22d of March, that the party set out from La Ciudad de los Angeles (the city of the Angels) in the southern part of Upper California, to proceed, in the shortest time, to Monterey on the Pacific coast, distant full four hundred miles The way is over a mountainous country, much of it uninhabited, with no other road than a trace, and many defiles to pass, particularly the maritime defile of *el Rincon* or Punto Gordo, fifteen miles in extent, made by the jutting of a precipitous mountain into the sea, and which can only be passed when the tide is out and the sea calm, and then in many places through the waves. The towns of Santa Barbara and San Luis Obispo, and occasional ranches, are the principal inhabited places on the route. Each of the party had three horses, nine in all, to take their turns under the saddle. The six loose horses ran ahead, without bridle or halter, and required some attention to keep to the track. When wanted for a change, say at the distance of twenty miles, they were caught by the *lasso*, thrown either by Don Jesus or the servant Jacob, who, though born in Washington, in his long expeditions with Colonel Fremont, had become as expert as a Mexican with the lasso, as sure as the mountaineer with the rifle, equal to either on horse or foot, and always a lad of courage and fidelity.

"None of the horses were shod, that being a practise unknown to the Californians. The most usual gait was a sweeping gallop. The first day they ran one hundred and twenty-five miles passing the San Fernando mountain, the defile of the Rincon, several other mountains, and slept at the hospitable ranche of Don Thomas Robberis, beyond the town of Santa Barbara. The only fatigue complained of in this day's ride, was in Jacob's right arm, made tired by throwing the lasso, and using it as a whip to keep the loose horses to the track.

"The next day they made another one hundred and twenty-five miles, passing the formidable mountain of Santa Barbara, and counting upon it the skeletons of some fifty horses, part of near double that number which perished in the crossing of that terrible mountain, by the California battalion, on Christmas day, 1846, amidst a raging tempest, and a deluge of rain and cold more killing than that of the Sierra Nevada—the day of severest suffering, say Fremont and his men, that they have ever passed. At sunset, the party stopped to sup with the friendly Captain Dana, and at nine at night San Luis Obispo was reached, the home of Don Jesus, and where an affecting reception awaited Lieutenant-Colonel Fremont, in consequence of an incident which occurred there that history will one day record; and he was detained till 10 o'clock in the morning receiving the visits of the inhabitants, (mothers and children included,) taking a breakfast of honor, and waiting for a relief of fresh horses to be brought in from the surrounding country. Here the nine horses from Los Angeles were left, and eight others taken in their place, and a Spanish boy added to the party to assist in managing the loose horses.

"Proceeding at the usual gait till eight at night, and having made some seventy miles, Don Jesus, who had spent the night before with his family and friends, and probably with but little sleep, became fatigued, and proposed a halt for a few hours. It was in the valley of the Salinas (salt river called *Buena Ventura* in the old maps,) and the haunt of marauding Indians. For safety during their repose, the party turned off the trace, issued through a *cañon* into a thick wood, and laid down, the horses being put to grass at a short distance, with the Spanish boy in the saddle to watch. Sleep, when commenced, was too sweet to be easily given up, and it was half-way between midnight and day, when the sleepers were aroused by an *estampedo* among the horses, and the calls of the boy. The cause of the alarm was soon found, not Indians, but white bears—

this valley being their great resort, and the place where Colonel Fremont and thirty-five of his men encountered some hundred of them the summer before, killing thirty upon the ground.

"The character of these bears is well known, and the bravest hunters do not like to meet them without the advantage of numbers. On discovering the enemy, Colonel Fremont felt for his pistols, but Don Jesus desired him to lie still, saying that 'people could scare bears;' and immediately hallooed at them in Spanish, and they went off. Sleep went off also; and the recovery of the horses frightened by the bears, building a rousing fire, making a breakfast from the hospitable supplies of San Luis Obispo, occupied the party till daybreak, when the journey was resumed. Eighty miles, and the afternoon brought the party to Monterey.

"The next day, in the afternoon, the party set out on their return, and the two horses rode by Colonel Fremont from San Luis Obispo, being a present to him from Don Jesus, he (Don Jesus) desired to make an experiment of what one of them could do. They were brothers, one a grass younger than the other, both of the same color, (cinnamon,) and hence called *el cañalo*, or *los cañalos*, (the cinnamon or the cinnamona.) The elder was to be taken for the trial; and the journey commenced upon him at leaving Monterey, the afternoon well advanced Thirty miles under the saddle done that evening, and the party stopped for the night. In the morning, the elder cañalo was again under the saddle for Colonel Fremont, and for ninety miles he carried him without a change, and without apparent fatigue. It was still thirty miles to San Luis Obispo, where the night was to be passed, and Don Jesus insisted that cañalo could do it, and so said the horse by his looks and action. But Colonel Fremont would not put him to the trial, and, shifting the saddle to the younger brother, the elder was turned loose to run the remaining thirty miles without a rider. He did so, immediately taking the lead and keeping it all the way, and entering San Luis in a sweeping gallop, nostrils distended, snuffing the air, and neighing with exultation at his return to his native pastures; his younger brother all the time at the head of the horses under the saddle, bearing on his bit, and held in by his rider. The whole eight horses made their one hundred and twenty miles each that day, (after thirty the evening before,) the elder cinnamon making ninety of his under the saddle that day besides thirty under the saddle the evening before; nor was there the least doubt that he would have done the whole distance in the same time if he had continued under the saddle.

"After a hospitable detention of another half a day at San Luis Obispo, the party set out for Los Angeles, on the same nine horses which they had rode from that place, and made the ride back in about the same time they had made it up, namely, at the rate of 125 miles a day.

"On this ride, the grass on the road was the food for the horses. At Monterey they had barley; but these horses, meaning those *trained and domesticated*, as the cañalos were, eat almost anything of vegetable food, or even drink, that their master uses, by whom they are petted and caressed, and rarely sold. Bread, fruit sugar, coffee, and even wine, (like the Persian horses,) they take from the hand of their master, and obey with like docility his slightest intimation. A tap of the whip on the saddle springs them into action; the check of a thread rein (on the Spanish bit) would stop them: and stopping short at speed they do not jostle the rider or throw him forward. They leap on anything—man, beast, or weapon, on which their master directs them. But this description, so far as conduct and behavior are concerned, of course only applies to the trained and domesticated horse."

CHAPTER XXX.

During the autumn of 1846, Fremont had had no time to visit his Mariposa purchase; but in the winter, while at Los Angeles, inviting Carson and Godey and two of his Delaware Indians, and his constant attendant Dobson, to take a tramp with him for hunting, in the time of sunny skies in February, he extended his hunt thither, and accomplished the discovery that he had a well-wooded and well-watered—for California well watered—tract of land, of exceeding beauty, clothed, as it was at this season, with a countless variety of flowering plants, these being the grasses of the country, and seemingly well adapted for tillage, certainly an excellent spot for an immense cattle ranche. They killed deer and antelope and smaller game, and with the lasso captured a score of wild horses from a drove of hundreds that fled at their approach; returning to Los Angeles within a week from the time of their departure, laden with the spoils of the chase.

Nor could these busy men refuse the kindly

hospitalities tendered them by the old and wealthy natives of Los Angeles. We have described their style of life as Carson had witnessed it in 1828; and now at a ball given by Don Pio Pico—for the *fandango* of the Mexican is a part of his life, and with all his reverses of fortune it must come in for its place —Carson and Fremont are of course guests, and Lieutenant Gillespie, and some other of the American officers. As the company was a mixed one, we will not attempt a description, but quote from Bayard Taylor's California, a scene of a similar kind at the close of the Constitutional Convention, about two years later when, with the discovery of gold, California had a population sufficient to demand a State government, and made one for herself, and prepared to knock for admission into the Union of States. In this Convention were the old fathers of California, American army officers, and some more recent arrivals; and well was it for California that the steps for the organization of her State government were taken so early, when the fact of Mexicans and natives having a claim was not ignored, as it might have been at a later date by the reckless adventurers who thronged the golden shore.

But it is only the ball at the close of the Convention we propose to describe, at which Colonel Fremont and David C. Broderick were present, as members of the Convention.

"The morning Convention was short and adjourned early yesterday, on account of a ball given by the Convention to the citizens of Monterey. The members, by a contribution of $25 each, raised the sum of $1,100 to provide for the entertainment, which was got up in return for that given by the citizens about four weeks since.

"The Hall was cleared of the forms and tables, and decorated with young pines from the forest. At each end were the American colors tastefully disposed across the boughs. Then chandeliers, neither of bronze or cut-glass, but neat and brilliant withal, poured their light upon the festivities. At eight o'clock—the fashionable hour in Monterey—the guests began to assemble, and in an hour afterward the Hall was crowded with nearly all the Californian and American residents. There were sixty ladies present, and an equal number of gentlemen, in addition to the members of the Convention. The dark-eyed daughters of Monterey, Los Angeles, and Santa Barbara mingled in pleasing contrast with the fairer bloom of the trans-Nevadian belles. The variety of feature and complexion was fully equaled by the variety of dress. In the whirl of the waltz, a plain, dark, nun-like robe would be followed by one of pink satin and gauze ; next, perhaps, a bodice of scarlet velvet, with gold buttons, and then a rich figured brocade, such as one sees on the stately dames of Titian.

" The dresses of the gentlemen showed considerable variety, but were much less picturesque. A complete ball-dress was a happiness attained only by a fortunate few, many appearing in borrowed robes.

" The appearance of the company, nevertheless, was genteel and respectable ; and perhaps the genial, unrestrained social spirit, that possessed all present, would have been less, had there been more uniformity of costume. General Riley was there in full uniform, with the yellow sash he wore at Contreras ; Majors Canby, Hill, and Smith, Captains Burton, and Kane, and the other officers stationed at Montery, accompanying him. In one group might be seen Captain Sutter's soldierly mustache and blue eye, in another the erect figure and quiet, dignified bearing of General Vallejos ; Don

Peblo de la Guerra, with his handsome, aristocratic features, was the floor manager, and gallantly discharged his office. Conspicuous among the members were Don Miguel de Rodrazena and Jacinto Rodriguez, both polished gentlemen and deservedly popular. Dominguez, the Indian member, took no part in the dance, but evidently enjoyed the scene as much as any one present. The most interesting figure to me was that of Padre Remisez, who, in his clerical cassock, looked on until a late hour. If the strongest advocate of priestly gravity and decorum had been present, he could not have found in his heart to grudge the good old padre the pleasure that beamed from his honest countenance.

"The band consisted of two violins and two guitars, whose music made up in spirit what it lacked in skill. They played, as it seemed to me, but three pieces alternately, for waltz, contra-dance, and quadrille. The latter dance was evidently an unfamiliar one, for once or twice the music ceased in the middle of the figure The etiquette of the dance was marked by that grave, stately courtesy, which has been handed down from the old Spanish times. The gentlemen invariably gave the ladies their hand to lead them to their places on the floor; in the pauses of the dance both parties stood motionless side by side, and at the conclusion the lady was gravely led back to her seat.

"At twelve o'clock supper was announced. The Court room in the lower story had been fitted up for the purpose, and as it was not large enough to admit all the guests, the ladies were first conducted thither, and waited upon by a select committee. The refreshments consisted of turkey, roast-pig, beef, tongue, and *patés*, with wines and liquors of various sorts, and coffee. A large supply had been provided, but after everybody was served, there was not much remaining. The ladies began to leave about two o'clock, but an hour later the dance was still going on with spirit."

The dance at the home of Pico was after the same fashion—and similar to those we have mentioned as the constant amusement of the people at Taos, where Carson resided, and in all the Mexican cities.

But Carson was too valuable an aid to be long allowed to be idle. In March, 1847, he was ordered to be the bearer of important despatches to the War Department at Washington, and Lieutenant Beale was directed to accompany nim with despatches for the Department of the Navy. The latter was still so much an invalid as to require Carson to lift him on and off his horse for the first twenty days of the journey, but Carson's genial spirits and kindly care, with the healthful exercise of horsemanship, recovered him rapidly; and the country was so well known to Carson that they avoided collisions with the Indians by eluding their haunts; except once upon the Gila, when they were attacked in the night, and a shower of arrows sent among them as they lay in camp, from which his men had escaped, being injured by holding their pack-saddles before them. They stopped briefly at Taos, and pursued their journey so rapidly that the two thousand five hundred miles on horseback, and the fifteen hundred by railroad, were accomplished in less than three months.

The incidents of such a journey had become every-day scenes to Carson, so that their narration would seem to him a waste of words on the part of his biographer. And yet the emotions with which he witnessed, for the first time, the monument of advancing civilization in the Eastern cities, and the zest with which he enjoyed the social comforts of the hospitality afforded him at the homes of Lieutenant Beale and Colonel Benton, can be better imagined than described. He had taken but a small supply of provisions from Los Angeles, lest it should be cumbersome to him, and as the road lay often through a country destitute of game, there had been fasting on the way, sometimes days together; but his party, which he had selected making their ability to endure such an enter prise a leading quality of commendation to him, bore all without a murmur; stimulated by the one impulse, of reaching their homes and friends, while Carson cared to secure the approbation of those whom he served, and the consciousness of having been an honor to his country.

Colonel Benton met him at St. Louis, and reaching Washington, Mrs. Fremont was at the depot to take him to hers and her father's home. She waited for no introduction, but at once approached him, calling him by name, and telling him she should have known him from her husband's description. After a brief tarry in Washington, a lion himself and introduced to all the lions, he departed with Lieutenant Beale for St. Louis, but business detained the latter who went later by sea; while Carson, whom

President Polk had made a Lieutenant in the army, with fifty troops under his command to take through the Comanche country, again commenced his journey across the prairies, having a battle with these Indians as was expected, for they were at war with the whites.

This did not occur, however, until near the Rocky Mountains, near the place called "The Point of Rocks," on the Santa Fé trail, which place is regarded as one of the most dangerous in the New Mexican country, because affording shelter for ambush at a place where the travel has to pass a spur of rocky hills, at whose base is found the water and camp-ground travelers seek, and where unwritten history counts many a battle.

Arriving here, Carson found a company of United States volunteers, and went into camp near them. Early in the morning the animals of the volunteer company were captured by a band of Indians, while the men were taking them to a spot of fresh pasture. The herders were without arms, and in the confusion the cattle came into Carson's camp, who, with his men, were ready with their rifles, and recaptured the cattle from the Indians, but the horses of the picketing party were successfully stampeded

Several of the thieves had been mortally wounded, as the signs after their departure showed, but the Indian custom of tying the wounded upon their horses, prevented taking the Indian's trophy of victory, the scalp, and the object of the Indians in their assaults. The success of the Arab-like Comanches is well illustrated by this skirmish, giving best assurance that Carson, who was never surprised in this whole journey, possessed that element of caution so requisite in a commander in such a country.

Of the two soldiers whose turn it had been to stand guard this morning, it was found that one was sleeping when the alarm was given, and when it was reported to Carson, he at once administered the Chinook method of punishment—the dress of a squaw—for that day, and resuming his journey, arrived safely in Santa Fé, where he left the soldiers, and hired sixteen men of his own choosing, to take with him the remainder of the journey, as he had been ordered at Fort Leavenworth. To his great joy, his family were here to meet him, as he had requested. Upon Virgin River, he had to command the obedience of Indians who came into his camp and left it tardily, by firing upon them, which required some nerve and experience in a leader of so small a party, while the Indians numbered three hundred warriors. They arrived at Los Angeles without further incident than the killing and eating of two mules, to eke out their scanty subsistence, in the destitution of game and time to hunt it; whence Carson proceeded to Monterey, to deliver his despatches at headquarters, and returned to the duty assigned to him as an acting Lieutenant in the United States Army, in the company of dragoons under Captain Smith, allowing him no time to recruit; and soon he was sent with a command of twenty-five dragoons, to the Tejon Pass, to examine the papers and cargoes of Indians passing this point, the route which most of the Indian depredators took in passing in and out of California; and here he did much good service during the winter.

In the spring he again went overland to Washington with despatches, meeting no serious difficulty till he came to the Grand River, where in the time of spring flood he was obliged to construct a raft, and the second load over was swamped, the men barely saving their lives, which rendered his party destitute of comforts in their onward journey, but arriving at Taca he stopped with his family, and at his own home gave his men a few days to recruit, and himself the luxury of intercourse with his family and friends, which no one enjoyed more than Christopher Carson.

They had encountered several hundred Indians of the Apaches and Utahs, whom Carson told he had nothing to give, and upon whom the appearance of his men gave assurance they would make little by attacking. At Santa Fé, Carson learned that his appointment as Lieutenant by the President had not been confirmed by the Senate, and his friends advised him not to carry the despatches any further; but Carson was not to be deterred from doing his duty because the honor he deserved was not accorded to him, saying that "as he had been selected for an important trust, he should do his best to fulfil it, if it cost him his life;" and he proceeded to Washington, feeling that if ill-usage had reached him in connection with Fremont, to whom he had been of so much service, it was no more than he might have expected; as, for many months past, political considerations and rivalries had been seen by him to govern the actions of certain men. instead of a care for the best interests of the country. He had seen mer in command of troops in the prairies who had the least possible knowledge of the country, and especially of Indian warfare. He would have advised that frontier men be chosen for such appointments, rather than those simply educated in the schools and entirely unaccustomed to endure privations, but if others neglected the wiser course, that was no reason why he should not do his duty.

Learning that the Comanches were upon the Santa Fé road, several hundred strong, he reduced his escort to ten choice mountain men, and determined upon making a trail of his own returned to Taos, and struck over to the headwaters of the Platte, and past Fort Kearney to Leavenworth, where he left his escort and proceeded alone to Washington, and delivering his despatches as directed, returned immediately to Leavenworth, and thence to Taos, where he arrived in October; and was again at home and free from the burdens and responsibilities of public life, with the settled purpose of making a protracted stay, and providing himself with a permanent home.

Perhaps there is no tribe of Indians besides the Seminoles in Florida, that have given the United States more trouble than the Apaches in the time that we have held the claim of their country; and the best proof of their bravery may be found in the fact that the warriors nearly all die in battle. Living in a country as healthy as any in the world, and constantly occupied in hunting buffalo, or Mexicans and whites, with whom they are at war, they are exceedingly regardful of their national honor, and as their mountain retreats are almost inaccessible, they have the advantage of regular troops, and almost of old mountaineers, only as the latter can equal them in numbers.

Colonel Beale was occupying this department at the time of which we write, and engaged in an effort to chastise the Apaches under *Clico Velasquez*, their exceedingly bloodthirsty and cruel chief, whose habit was to adorn his dress with the finger bones of the victims he had slaughtered. Colonel Beale took charge of the command himself, and employed Carson as his guide. They crossed snow mountains to search for the Indians, and returning came upon a village, which they attacked, and captured a large amount of goods and two of the chiefs of the tribe, with whom Colonel Beale had a long talk, and then dismissed to return to their tribe hoping thus to convince them of the magna nimity of the United States Government, when the command returned to Taos to recruit his troops.

Meantime Carson entertained, at his own home in Taos, Fremont and his party of suffering explorers, who were making a winter survey of a pass for a road to California, and by taking a difficult mountain pass, had lost all their mules and several of their party. Science is not all that is needed for such undertakings, and as labor and learning should act in copartnership, to be most effective, so theoretic and practical skill should be associated in any effort of difficulty, as this trip of Colonel Fremont, without an experienced mountaineer for a guide, proved to him and his men, some of whom had fed upon the others who had starved.

CHAPTER XXXI.

In the last chapter, we left Fremont in the hospitable mansion of his old and tried friend Carson, after one of the most extraordinary journeys ever performed by any man who survived to tell its horrors; and as the names of Carson and Fremont are inseparably cemented in history, as in friendship, and as the former had often endured sufferings almost as great as those of his old commander and friend, we shall be pardoned if we allude to this journey at some length. There is no earthly doubt that had Carson been the guide, many valuable lives of noble, glorious men might have been spared, and sufferings on the part of those who survived this disastrous expedition, almost too horrible for belief, avoided.

Colonel Fremont, in a letter written to his wife from Taos, the day after his arrival there in a famishing condition, and having lost one full third of his party by absolute starvation and freezing, mentions that at Pueblo he engaged as a guide, an old trapper of twenty-five years' experience, named "Bill Williams," and he frankly admits that the "error of his journey was committed in engaging this man."

In narrating some of the incidents of this terribly disastrous journey, we shall use, of course, the language of those best qualified to depict its horrors, *i. e.*, Colonel Fremont, and Mr. Carvalho, a gentleman of Baltimore, who accompanied the expedition as daguerreotypist and artist.

Colonel Fremont, in his letter to his wife, treats of the subject generally, but when we quote from the narrative of Mr. Carvalho, we think our readers will admit that such a record of human suffering and human endurance, added to such an exhibition of moral and physical courage, has never been paralleled.

Colonel Fremont writes (speaking first of Williams the guide):

"He proved never to have in the least known, or entirely to have forgotten, the whole region of country through which we were to pass. We occupied more than half a month in making the journey of a few days, blundering a tortuous way through deep snow which already began to choke up the passes, for which we were obliged to waste time in searching. About the 11th December we found ourselves at the North of the Del Norte Cañon, where that river issues from the St. John's Mountain, one of the highest, most rugged and impracticable of all the Rocky Mountain ranges, inaccessible to trappers and hunters even in the summer time.

"Across the point of this elevated range our guide conducted us, and having still great confidence in his knowledge, we pressed onwards with fatal resolution. Even along the river bottoms the snow was already belly deep for the mules, frequently snowing in the valley and almost constantly in the mountains. The cold was extraordinary; at the warmest hours of the day (between one and two) the thermometer (Fahrenheit) standing in the shade of only a tree trunk at zero; the day sunshiny, with a moderate breeze. We pressed up towards the summit, the snow deepening; and in four or five days we reached the naked ridges which lie above the timbered country, and which form the dividing grounds between the waters of the Atlantic and Pacific oceans

"Along these naked ridges it storms nearly all winter, and the winds sweep across them with remorseless fury. On our first attempt to cross we encountered a *pouderié* (dry snow driven thick through the air by violent wind, and in which objects are visible only at a short distance), and were driven back, having some ten or twelve men variously frozen, face, hands, or feet. The guide became nigh being frozen to death here, and dead mules were already lying about the fires. Meantime, it snowed steadily. The next day we made mauls, and beating a road or trench through the snow crossed the crest in defiance of the *pouderié* and encamped immediately below in the edge of the timber.

"Westward, the country was buried in deep snow. It was impossible to advance, and to turn back was equally impracticable. We were overtaken by sudden and inevitable ruin and it was instantly apparent that we should lose every animal.

"I determined to recross the mountain more towards the open country, and haul or pack the baggage (by men) down to the Del Norte. With great labor the baggage was transported across the crest to the head springs of a little stream leading to the main river. A few days were sufficient to destroy our fine band of mules.

They generally kept huddled together, and as they froze, one would be seen to tumble down, and the snow would cover him; some times they would break off and rush down towards the timber until they were stopped by the deep snow, where they were soon hidden by the *pouderié*.

"The courage of the men failed fast; in fact, I have never seen men so soon discouraged by misfortune as we were on this occasion; but, as you know, the party was not constituted like the former ones. But among those who deserve to be honorably mentioned, and who behaved like what they were—men of the old exploring party,—were Godey, King, and Taplin; and first of all Godey.

"In this situation, I determined to send in a party to the Spanish settlements of New Mexico for provisions and mules to transport our baggage to Taos. With economy, and after we should leave the mules, we had not two weeks' provisions in the camp. These consisted of a store which I had reserved for a hard day, macaroni and bacon. From among the volunteers I chose King, Brackenridge, Creutzfeldt, and the guide Williams; the party under the command of King. In case of the least delay at the settlements, he was to send me an express.

"Day after day passed by, and no news from our express party. Snow continued to fall almost incessautly on the mountain. The spirits of the camp grew lower. Prone laid down in the trail and froze to death. In a sunshiny day, and having with him means to make a fire, he threw his blankets down in the trail and laid there till he froze to death. After sixteen days had elapsed from King's departure, I became so uneasy at the delay that I decided to wait no longer. I was aware that our troops had been engaged in hostilities with the Spanish Utahs and Apaches, who range in the North River valley, and became fearful that they (King's party) had been cut off by these Indians; I could imagine no other accident. Leaving the camp employed with the baggage and in charge of Mr. Vincenthaler, I started down the river with a small party consisting of Godey (with his young nephew), Mr. Preuss and Saunders. We carried our arms and provision for two or three days. In the camp the messes had provisions for two or three meals, more or less; and about five pounds of sugar to each man. Failing to mee-

King, my intention was to make the Red River settlement about twenty-five miles north of Taos, and send back the speediest relief possible. My instructions to the camp were, that if they did not hear from me within a stated time, they were to follow down the Del Norte.

"About sunset on the sixth day, we discovered a little smoke, in a grove of timber off from the river, and thinking perhaps it might be our express party on its return, we went to see. This was the twenty-second day since they had left us, and the sixth since we had left the camp. We found them—three of them—Creutzfeldt, Brackenridge, and Williams—the most miserable objects I have ever seen. I did not recognize Creutzfeldt's features when Brackenridge brought him up to me and mentioned his name. They had been starving. King had starved to death a few days before. His remains were some six or eight miles above, near the river. By aid of the horses, we carried these three men with us to Red River settlement, which we reached (Jan. 20), on the tenth evening after leaving our camp in the mountains, having traveled through snow and on foot one hundred and sixty miles.

"The morning after reaching the Red River town, Godey and myself rode on to the Rio Hondo and Taos, in search of animals and supplies, and on the second evening after that on which we had reached Red River, Godey had returned to that place with about thirty animals, provisions, and four Mexicans, with which he set out for the camp on the following morning.

"You will remember that I had left the camp with occupation sufficient to employ them for three or four days, after which they were to follow me down the river. Within that time I had expected the relief from King, if it was to come at all.

"They remained where I had left them seven days, and then started down the river. Manuel —you will remember Manuel, the Cosumne Indian—gave way to a feeling of despair after they had traveled about two miles, begged Haler to shoot him, and then turned and made his way back to the camp; intending to die there, as he doubtless soon did. They followed our trail down the river—twenty-two men they were in all. About ten miles below the camp, Wise gave out, threw away his gun and blanket and a few hundred yards further fell over into the snow and died. Two Indian boys, young men, countrymen of Manuel, were behind. They rolled up Wise in his blanket, and buried him in the snow on the river bank. No more died that day—none the next. Carver raved during the night, his imagination wholly occupied with images of many things which he fancied himself eating. In the morning he wandered off from the party, and probably soon died. They did not see him again.

"Sorel on this day gave out, and laid down to die. They built him a fire, and Morin, who was in a dying condition, and snow-blind, remained. These two did not probably last till the next morning. That evening, I think, Hubbard killed a deer. They traveled on, getting here and there a grouse, but probably nothing else, the snow having frightened off the game. Things were desperate, and brought Haler to the determination of breaking up the party, in order to prevent them from living upon each other. He told them ' that he had done all he could for them, that they had no other hope remaining than the expected relief, and that their best plan was to scatter and make the best of their way in small parties down the river

That, for his part, if he was to be eaten, he would, at all events, be found traveling when he did die.' They accordingly separated.

"With Mr. Haler continued five others and the two Indian boys. Rohrer now became very despondent; Haler encouraged him by recalling to mind his family, and urged him to hold out a little longer. On this day he fell behind, but promised to overtake them at evening. Haler, Scott, Hubbard, and Martin agreed that if any one of them should give out, the others were not to wait for him to die, but build a fire for him, and push on. At night, Kern's mess encamped a few hundred yards from Haler's, with the intention, according to Taplin, to remain where they were until the relief should come, and in the meantime to live upon those who had died, and upon the weaker ones as they should die. With the three Kerns were Cathcart, Andrews, McKie, Stepperfeldt, and Taplin.

"Ferguson and Beadle had remained together behind. In the evening, Rohrer came up and remained with Kern's mess. Mr. Haler learned afterwards from that mess that Rohrer and Andrews wandered off the next day and died. They say they saw their bodies. In the morning Haler's party continued on. After a few hours, Hubbard gave out. They built him a fire, gathered him some wood, and left him without, as Haler says, turning their heads to look at him as they went off. About two miles further, Scott—you remember Scott—who used to shoot birds for you at the frontier—gave out. They did the same for him as for Hubbard, and continued on. In the afternoon, the Indian boys went ahead, and before nightfall met Godey with the relief. Haler heard and knew the guns which he fired for him at night, and starting early in the morning, soon met him. I heard that they all cried together like children. Haler turned back with Godey, and went with him to where they had left Scott. He was still alive, and was saved. Hubbard was dead—still warm. From Kern's mess they learned the death of Andrews and Rohrer, and a little above, met Ferguson, who told them that Beadle had died the night before."

Such is the portion of the brief, but thrilling, narrative of this extraordinary and disastrous journey, as detailed in a familiar letter by Colonel Fremont to his wife; but Mr. Carvalho gives in detail some of the particulars of the horrors which overtook them, all through the

LIFE OF KIT CARSON. 333

anfortunate error of engaging as guide a man who either knew nothing, or had forgotten all he had ever known, of the localities which the party designed and hoped to reach.

CHAPTER XXXII.

WE quote now from the closing part of Mr Carvalho's narrative:

"At last we are drawn to the necessity of killing our brave horses for food. To-day the first sacrifice was made. It was with us all a solemn event, rendered far more solemn however by the impressive scene which followed. Colonel Fremont came out to us, and after referring to the dreadful necessities to which his men had been reduced on a previous expedition, of eating each other, he begged us to swear that in no extremity of hunger would any of his men lift his hand against, or attempt to prey upon, a comrade; sooner let him die with them than live upon them. They all promptly took the oath, and threatened to shoot the first one that hinted or proposed such a thing.

"It was a most impressive scene, to witness twenty-two men on a snowy mountain, with bare heads, and hands and eyes upraised to heaven, uttering the solemn vow, 'So help me

God!'—and the valley echoed, 'So help me God!' I never, until that moment, realized the awful situation in which I was placed. I remembered the words of the Psalmist, and felt perfectly assured of my final safety. They *wandered in the wilderness* in *a solitary way; they found no city to dwell in. Hungry and thirsty their soul fainteth within them, and they cried unto the Lord in their trouble, and he delivered them out of their distresses.*

* * * * *

"When an animal gave out, he was shot down by the Indians, who immediately cut his throat, and saved all the blood in our camp kettle. This animal was divided into twenty-two parts. Two parts for Colonel Fremont and his cook, ten parts for the white camp, and ten parts for the Indians. Colonel Fremont hitherto messed with his officers; at this time he requested that they would excuse him, as it gave him pain, and called to mind the horrible scenes which had been enacted during his last expedition—he could not see his officers obliged to partake of such disgusting food.

"The rule he adopted was that one animal should serve for six meals for the whole party. If one gave out in the meantime, of course it was an exception; but otherwise, on no consideration was an animal to be slaughtered, for every one that was killed, placed a man on foot, and limited our chances of escape from our present situation. If the men chose to eat up their six meals all in one day, they would have to go without until the time arrived for killing another. It frequently happened that the white camp was without food from twenty-four to thirty-six hours, while Colonel Fremont and the Delawares always had a meal. The latter religiously abstained from encroaching on the portion allotted for another meal, while many men of our camp, I may say all of them, not content with their portion, would, to satisfy the cravings of hunger, surreptitiously purloin from their pile of meat, at different times, sundry pieces, thus depriving themselves of each other's allowance. My own sense of right was so subdued by the sufferings I endured by hunger, and walking almost barefooted through the snow, that while going to guard one night, I stole a piece of frozen horse liver, ate it raw, and thought it, at the time, the most delicious morsel I ever tasted.

"The entrails of the horse were 'well shaken (for we had no water to wash them in) and boiled with snow, producing a highly flavored soup, which the men considered so valuable and delicious that they forbade the cook to skim the pot for fear any portion of it might be lost. The hide was divided into equal portions, and with the bones roasted and burnt to a crisp. This we munched on the road; but the men not being satisfied with the division of the meat by the cook, made him turn his back, while another took up each share separately, and inquired who should have it. When the snows admitted it, we collected the thick leaves of a species of cactus which we also put in the fire to burn off the prickles, and ate. It then resembled in taste and nourishment an Irish potato peeling. We lived in this way for nearly fifty days, traveling from Grand River across the divide to Green River, and over the first range of the Wahsach Mountains, on foot, Colonel Fremont at our head, tramping a pathway for his men to follow. He, as well as the rest of the party, towards the last was entirely barefoot—some of them had a piece of raw hide on their feet, which, however, becoming hard and stiff by the frost, made them more uncomfortable than walking without any.

"Yesterday, Mr. Oliver Fuller, of St. Louis,

who had been on foot for some weeks, suddenly gave out. Our engineers and myself were with him. He found himself unable to proceed—the snow was very deep, and his feet were badly frozen. He insisted that we should leave him, and hasten to camp for relief; not being able to render him any assistance by remaining, we wrapped his blankets around him and left him on the trail. In vain we searched for material to build him a fire—nothing was visible but a wild waste of snow; we were also badly crippled, and we did not arrive in camp until ten o'clock at night, at which time it began snowing furiously. We told Colonel Fremont of Mr. Fuller's situation, when he sent a Mexican named Frank, with the two best animals and cooked horsemeat, to bring Mr. Fuller in. There was not a dry eye in the whole camp that night—the men sat up anxiously awaiting the return of our companions.

"At daylight, they being still out, Colonel Fremont sent three Delawares, mounted, to look for them. About ten o'clock one of them returned with the Mexican and two mules. Frank was badly frozen, he had lost the track, and bewildered and cold, he sank down holding on to the animals, where he was found by the Dela ware during the afternoon. The two Delawares supporting Mr. Fuller were seen approaching He was found awake, but almost dead from the cold and faintness. Colonel Fremont personally rendered him all the assistance in his power. So did all of us—for he was beloved and respected by the whole camp for his gentlemanly behavior and his many virtues. Colonel Fremont remained at this dreary place near three days, to allow poor Fuller time to recruit—and afterwards assigned to him the best mule to carry him, while two of the men walked on either side to support him. A portion of our scanty food was appropriated at every meal from each man's portion to make Mr. Fuller's larger, as he required sustenance more than they did.

"On the 7th February, almost in sight of succor, the Almighty took him to himself: he died on horseback—his two companions wrapped him in his india rubber blanket and laid him across the trail. We arrived next day at Parawan. After the men had rested a little, we went, in company with three or four of the inhabitants of Parawan, to bury our deceased friend. His remains had not been disturbed during our absence."

In the month of February, and soon after

Fremont's arrival and departure, Colonel Beale again solicited Carson to be his guide while he paid a visit to a large village of Indians congregated on the Arkansas, for the purpose of carrying out a stipulation of the treaty with Mexico, that the captives the Indians retained in the territory ceded to the United States should be returned to Mexico. He found four tribes congregated, to the number of two thousand, for the purpose of meeting their agent, an experienced mountaineer, who informed Colonel Beale that it would be useless to attempt to enforce the provisions of the treaty here, especially when so many Indians were together, and succeeded in persuading him to desist from the use of force against them.

These Indians had been accustomed to dealing with poorly clad Mexican soldiers, and the sight and bearing of Colonel Beale and Carson and the men under their command, must have induced a respect for the government they represented, so that they did not consider the expedition as without good result.

The Comanche Indians could not well have been induced to fulfil the provisions of the treaty with Mexico, especially as they were not a party to it, for in the very many years past, it had been their custom to make incursions upon the Mexican settlements and parties of travelers, and to capture their cattle and take their goods, besides bringing away as many children as possible, in order that the girls procured in this way should, when grown, marry the braves of the tribe; till now at least a third of the blood of the tribe was Mexican. This amalgamation had become more extensive in this than in any of the other New Mexican tribes.

The Apache is smaller in stature and more closely built than the Comanche; less skilled in horsemanship, but equally brave, with beautiful symmetry of form, and " muscles as hard as iron," with an elasticity of movement that shows a great amount of physical training, and an eye that reveals the treachery of their character.

CHAPTER XXXIII.

ARRIVING again in Taos, to carry into effect at once the resolution he had formed of establishing for himself a permanent home he joined his old friend Maxwell in the purpose of occupying a beautifully romantic mountain valley, fifty miles east of Taos, called by the Indians Rayedo, which would long since have been settled by the Mexicans, only it was very much exposed to Indian depredations.

Through the center of this valley flows a broad mountain stream, and, for the loveliness of the scenery, or the fertility of its broad, sloping basin, or the mountain supply of timber, there can scarcely be found a spot to equal it. Carson and Maxwell established a settlement about mid-way in the valley ; and at the present date, have an imposing little village, in which the houses of Carson and Maxwell are prominent by reason of their greater dimensions, and indicate to the trader a style of plenteous comfort, which, while it might offend the pale-faced denizen of our most fashionable thoroughfares, the traveler, who has learned to love nature and health, gazes upon with pleasure, and gladly tarries to enjoy the patriarchal hospitality, and the sumptuous, almost regal luxury of their hunter occupants, who " count their horses and their cattle by the hundreds," and whose thousand sheep are on the hills; whose larder is replenished from the still countless herds of prairie oxen which roam through those magnificent plains, and the lesser bands of speed-defying, beauteous quadrupeds of the hills, and the fleet climbers of the rocks and big-horned mountain cliffs, and the flocks that build their eyrie in their crags, all of which are occupants of the sheep-pastures of these chevaliers of the wilderness, and in whose court-yards may be seen specimens of this game, of which they are not ashamed; for a young Carson has lassoed a little grizzly, while antelope and young fawn feed from his sister's fingers.

Here too the Indian braves fear not to come and call the master of the mansion, Father,— "Father Kit," is his long time appellation— and they have learned to look on him and his, with all that reverence and fondness with which grateful children look upon a worthy sire.

Carson cannot tarry at his pleasant home, much more than to care for its necessary superintendence, for his life is the property of the public; and to the quiet settlement of the Indians into the condition which is happiest for them, so far as it can be secured in the condition of the country and their own habitudes, is the work to which he has wisely devoted himself. He has given to the Indians the best years of his ever busy life, and gives them still, neglectful of immediate personal comfort —or rather finding highest satisfaction in doing what is fittest he should do, because it is the work in which he can accomplish the most good.

In the vicinity of the home of Carson, and that of his friend Maxwell, are gathered a number of their old comrades—men of the mountains, who have survived the multitudinous and conflicting events which have come over the spirit of the Yankee, and the activities of the Yankee nations, since the business of trapping first became for her hardy sons a lucrative employment; and here, in the society of each other, and the conscious security of pro tection for each other, in a locality congenial to their tastes, with occasional old time occupations, and where the rivalries of their predilections can be still indulged, and quietly maintained, they are-ever ready after every test to concede to Christopher Carson the palm of being *first* as a hunter, *first* as an experienced traveler and guide through the mountain country, whether it be by a route he has, or one he has never before traveled.

The stories of his exploits in defense of his neighbors and friends, and to recover from the Indians property they had stolen, since he left the service of the Army of the United States, would of themselves fill a volume, and we have space to allude to but a very few.

A Mrs. White, the wife of a merchant of Santa Fé, had been taken captive with her child, (which was soon killed before her eyes), by a party of Apaches, who had shot her husband, and all the men of his company, before capturing her. A party of New Mexicans was at once organized to pursue the Indian band, and effect Mrs. White's release if possible. The guidance of this party was entrusted to a neighbor by the name of Watkins Leroux, rather than to Carson. They found the Apache murderers, and Carson was advancing foremost to attack them, when he discovered that the rest of the party were not following; consequently he had to retire, and when the commander ordered the attack to be made, it was too late, for the Indians had murdered Mrs. White and were preparing to escape by flight. Carson tells this story with all the generous magnanimity a great soul exercises in speaking of a failure on the part of a rival; admitting that, if his advice had been followed, they might have saved Mrs. White, but affirming that the command "did what seemed to it the best, and therefore no one has any right to find fault."

This occurred in the autumn of eighteen hundred and forty-nine, directly after the commencement of the settlement of Rayedo.

Near the close of the following winter, all the animals belonging to the party of ten dragoons which had been stationed there to protect the settlement, were run off by the marauding Apaches, and the two herders having them in charge were wounded. Early the following morning, Carson and three of the settlers with the ten dragoons, started in pursuit, discovered the Indians—twenty well-armed warriors—and four of the party being obliged to stop, because their animals had given out, the remaining ten rode down the Indians, who might themselves have escaped but for their persistence in retaining the stolen horses, which were all recaptured except four, while five of the warriors were killed, and several more wounded. This expedition was planned and executed under the direction of Carson, and the fact that he was their leader gave every man confidence, as they knew that with him an engagement implied success or death.

The next spring Carson went to Fort Laramie with a drove of horses and mules, making the journey successfully and pleasantly in company with Timothy Goodell, another old mountaineer, being the observed of all observers to the large numbers of overland emigrants to California whom he met at the fort, where Goodell left him to go to California.

Carson found a Mexican to attend him upon his return, and taking a circuitous course, he managed to avoid the Apaches; often traveling by moonlight, and taking their animals into a quiet nook, and climbing a tree for a little sleep during the day, they finally reached the Mexican settlements in safety.

The days of the following summer winged their happy flight with great rapidity, while Carson was directing and aiding in his farming, and, of course, pursuing his favorite employment of hunting, ever returning from a hunt with his horse laden with deer or antelope, wild turkey and ducks, or perhaps a half score or more of prairie chickens, to complete the list. Only once was his work interrupted by the harsher business of chastising offenders against justice, and this time the guilty parties were two white men.

A party of desperadoes, so frequently the nuisance of a new country, had formed a plot to murder and rob two wealthy citizens, whom they had volunteered to accompany to the settlements in the States, and were already many miles on their way, when Carson was informed of the nefarious design. In one hour he had organized a party, and was on his way in quick pursuit, taking a more direct route to intercept the party, and endeavoring at the same time to avoid the vicinity of the Indians, who were now especially hostile, but of whose movements Carson was as well informed as any one could be. In two days out from Taos, they came upon a camp of United States recruits, whose officer volunteered to accompany him with twenty men, which offer was accepted, and by forced marches they soon overtook the party of traders, and at once arrested Fox, the leader of the wretches, and then proceeded to inform Messrs. Brevoort and Weatherhead of the danger which they had escaped; and they, though at first astounded by the disclosure, had noticed many things to convince them that the plot would soon have been put in execution.

Taking the members of their party whom they knew were trusty, they at once ordered the rest, thirty-five in number, to leave immediately, except Fox, who remained in charge of Carson, to whom the traders were abundant in their thanks for his timely interference in their behalf, and who refused every offer of recompense.

Fox was taken to Taos, and imprisoned for a number of months; but as a crime only in intent was difficult to be proved, and the *adobe* walls of their houses were not secure enough to retain one who cared to release himself, Fox was at last liberated, and went to parts unknown

On the return of Messrs. Brevoort and Weatherhead from St. Louis, they presented Carson with a magnificent pair of pistols, upon whose silver mounting were inscribed such words as would laconically illustrate his noble deed, and the appreciation of the donors of the great service rendered.

The summer following was consumed in an excursion for trade, on behalf of himself and Maxwell, and a visit to the home of his daughter, now married in St. Louis; and which was prosecuted without incident worthy of note, until he came to a Cheyenne village on the Arkansas, upon his return. This village had received an affront from the officer of a party of United States troops bound to New Mexico, who had whipped one of their chiefs, some ten days before the arrival of Carson; and to have revenge upon some one of the whites, was now the passion of the whole tribe.

The conduct of this officer is only a specimen of that which thousands have exercised toward the Indians of the different tribes; and the result is the same in all cases. Carson's was the first party to pass the Indian village after this insult; and so many years had elapsed since he was a hunter at Bent's Fort, and so much had this nation been stirred by their numberless grievances, that Carson's name was no longer a talisman of safety to his party, nor

even of respect to himself, in their then state of
excitement; and as Carson went deliberately
into the war council, which the Indians were
holding on the discovery of his party, having
ordered his men to keep their force close together,
the Indians supposing he could not
understand them, continued to talk freely of
the manner of capturing the effects, and killing
the whole party, and especially himself, whom
they at once concluded was the leader. When
Kit had heard all their plans, he coolly addressed
them in the Cheyenne language, telling
them who he was, his former association with
and kindness to their tribe; and that now, he
should be glad to render them any assistance
they might need; but as to their having his
scalp, he should claim the right of saying a
word. The Indians departed, and Carson went
on his way; but there were hundreds of the
Cheyennes in sight upon the hills, and though
they made no attack, Carson knew he was in
their power, nor had they given up the idea of
taking his train. His cool deliberation kept
his men in spirits, and yet, except upon two
or three of the whole fifteen, he could place
no reliance in an emergency. At night the men
and mules were all brought within the circle

of wagons, grass was cut with their sheath knives, and brought into the mules, and as large a guard was placed as possible. When all was quiet, Carson called outside the camp with him a Mexican boy of the party, and explaining to him the danger which threatened them, told him it was in his power to save the lives of the company, and giving him instructions how to proceed, sent him on alone to Rayedo, a journey of nearly three hundred miles, to ask an escort of United States troops to be sent out to meet him, telling the brave young Mexican to " put a good many miles between him and the camp before morning;" and so he started him, with a few rations of provisions, without telling the rest of the party that such a step was necessary. This boy had long been in Carson's service, and was well known to him as faithful and active, so that he had no doubts as to the faithful execution of the trust confided to him; and in a wild country like New Mexico, with the outdoor life and habits of its people, a journey like the one on which he was despatched, was not an unusual occurrence: indeed, in that country, parties on foot often accompany those on horse, for days together, and do not seem to feel the fatigue

Carson now returned to the camp to watch all night himself; and at break of day they were again upon the road. No Indians appeared until nearly noon, when five warriors came galloping toward them. As they came near enough to hear him, Carson ordered them to halt, and approaching, told them that the night before, he had sent a messenger to Rayedo, to inform the troops that their tribe were annoying him; and if he or his men were molested, terrible punishment would be inflicted by those who would surely come to his relief. The Indians replied, that they would look for the moccasin tracks, which they probably found, and Carson considered this the reason that induced the whole village to pass away toward the hills after a little time, evidently seeking a place of safety. The young Mexican overtook the party of troops whose officer had caused the trouble, to whom he told his story, and failing to secure sympathy, he continued to Rayedo, and procured thence immediate assistance. Major Grier despatched a party of troops, under Lieutenant R. Johnston, which, making rapid marches, met Carson twenty-five miles below Bent's Fort; and, though they encountered no Indians, the effect of the quick transit of troops from one part of the country to another, could not be other than good, as a means of impressing the Indians with the effective force of the United States troops.

CHAPTER XXXIV.

EIGHTEEN years had elapsed, full of eventful history—especially the last ten—since Carson had renounced the business of trapping, and of late there had been an almost irrepressible longing once more to try his skill at his old employment, in company with others who had been, with himself, adepts at the business. Accordingly he and Maxwell, by a great effort, succeeded in collecting sixteen more of their old companions, and taking care to provide themselves abundantly with all the necessaries for such a service, and with such added articles of comfort as the pleasurable character of the excursion dictated, they started, with Carson at the head of the band, " any one of whom would have periled his life for any other, and having voted that the expedition should be one for hard work, as when they trapped for gain long ago," they dashed on across the plains, till they came to the South Platte, and upon its well remembered waters, formed their camp and set their traps, having first apprised themselves, by the "signs," that the beaver were abundant. Indeed, so long ago had trapping gone into disuse, that the hunt proved successful beyond their anticipations, and they worked down this stream, through the Laramie plains to the New Park, on to the Old Park, and upon a large number of the streams, their old resorts, and returned to Rayedo with a large stock of furs, having enlivened the time by the recital to each other of many of the numberless entertaining events which had crowded upon their lives while they had been separated.

Would not the reader like to have made this excursion with them, and witnessed the infinite zest with which these mature and experienced men entered again upon what seemed now to them the sport of their earlier years? They made it, as much as possible, a season of enjoyment. One of the party had lassoed a grizzly, but, finding it inconvenient to retain him, he had been shot, and bear steaks, again enjoyed together, had been a part of the Fourth of July treat they afforded their visitors, the Sioux Indians. As we have but little further opportunity, we will quote Fremont's description of the Mountain Parks, for the sake of giving the reader an idea of the locality of this last trapping enterprise of Kit Carson:

"Our course in the afternoon brought us to the main Platte River, here a handsome stream, with a uniform breadth of seventy yards, except where widened by frequent islands. It was apparently deep, with a moderate current, and wooded with groves of large willow.

"The valley narrowed as we ascended, and presently degenerated into a gorge, through which the river passed as through a gate. We entered it, and found ourselves in the New Park—a beautiful circular valley of thirty miles diameter, walled in all round with snowy mountains, rich with water and with grass, fringed with pine on the mountain sides below the snow line, and a paradise to all grazing animals. The Indian name for it signifies " *cow lodge*," of which our own may be considered a translation; the enclosure, the grass, the water, and the herds of buffalo roaming over it, naturally presenting the idea of a park, 7,720 feet above tide water.

"It is from this elevated *cove*, and from the gorges of the surrounding mountains, and some lakes within their bosoms, that the Great Platte River collects its first waters, and assumes its first form; and certainly no river has a more beautiful origin.

"Descending from the pass, we found ourselves again on the western waters; and halted to noon on the edge of another mountain valley, called the Old Park, in which is formed Grand River, one of the principal branches of the Colorado of California. We were now moving with some caution, as, from the trail, we found the Arapahoe village had also passed this way. As we were coming out of their enemy's country, and this was a war ground, we were desirous to avoid them. After a long afternoon's march, we halted at night on a small creek, tributary to a main fork of Grand River, which ran through this portion of the valley. The appearance of the country in the Old Park is interesting, though of a different character from the New; instead of being a comparative plain, it is more or less broken into hills, and surrounded by the high mountains, timbered on the lower parts with quaking asp and pines.

"We entered the Bayou Salada, (South Park,) and immediately below us was a green valley, through which ran a stream; and a short distance opposite rose snowy mountains, whose summits were formed into peaks of naked rock.

"On the following day we descended the stream by an excellent buffalo trail, along the open grassy bottom of the river. On our right, the bayou was bordered by a mountainous range, crested with rocky and naked peaks; and below it had a beautiful park-like character of pretty level prairies, interspersed among low spurs, wooded openly with pine and quaking asp, contrasting well with the denser pines which swept around on the mountain sides.

"During the afternoon, Pike's Peak had been plainly in view before us.

"The next day we left the river, which continued its course towards Pike's Peak; and taking a southeasterly direction, in about ten miles we crossed a gentle ridge, and, issuing from the South Park, found ourselves involved among the broken spurs of the mountains which border the great prairie plains. Although broken and extremely rugged, the country was very interesting, being well watered by numerous affluents to the Arkansas River, and covered with grass and a variety of trees."

Carson had disposed of his furs, and was again quietly attending to his ranche, when he heard of the exorbitant prices for which sheep were selling in California, and determined to enter upon a speculation. He had already visited the Navajos Indians, and thither he went again, and in company with Maxwell and another mountaineer, purchased several thousand sheep; and with a suitable company of trusty men as shepherds, took them to Fort Laramie, and thence by the regular emigrant route, past Salt Lake to California, and arriving without any disaster, disposed of them in one of the frontier towns, and then went down to the Sacramento valley, to witness the change which had come over old familiar places; not that the mining did not interest him; he had seen that before in Mexico, but he had not seen the cities which had sprung into existence at a hundred points, in the foot-hills of the Sierras, nor had he seen San Francisco, that city of wondrous growth, which now contained thirty-five thousand inhabitants.

But for the remembrance of the hills on which the city rested, Carson would not have known the metropolis of California, as the spot where in '48 "the people could be counted in an hour." In San Francisco he met so many old friends, and so many, who, knowing him from the history of his deeds, desired to do him honor, that the attentions he received, while it gratified his ambition, were almost annoying.

Tired by the anxiety and hard work of bringing his property over a long and dangerous journey to a good market, he had looked for rest and retirement; but instead, he was everywhere sought out and made conspicuous.

He found himself surrounded with the choice spirits of the new El Dorado; his name a prestige of strength and position, and his society courted by everybody. The siren voice of pleasure failed not to speak in his ear her most flattering invitations. Good-fellowship took him incessantly by the hand, desiring to lead him into the paths of dissipation. But the gay vortex, with all its brilliancy, had no attractions for him; the wine cup, with its sparkling arguments, failed to convince his calm earnestness of character, that his simple habits of life needed remodeling. To the storm, however, he was exposed; but, like a good ship during the gale, he weathered the fierce blast, and finally took his departure from the new city of a day, with his character untarnished, but nevertheless leaving behind him many golden opinions.

Some newspaper scribbler, last autumn, an

nounced the death of Carson, and said, in connection, "His latest and *most remarkable exploit* on the plains was enacted in 1853, when he conducted a drove of sheep safely to California. Probably the writer was one of those whose eager curiosity had met a rebuff, in the quiet dignity with which Carson received the officiousness of the rabble who thronged around him on that visit. Not that he appreciated honor less, but that its unnecessary attachments were exceedingly displeasing to him.

In this terribly fast city, where the *monte* table, and its kindred dissipations, advertised themselves without a curtain, and where to indulge was the rule rather than the exception, Carson was able to stand fire, for he had been before now tried by much greater temptations.

In the strange commingling of people from all quarters of the globe, whom Carson witnessed in San Francisco, he saw but a slight exaggeration of what he had often witnessed in Santa Fé,—and indeed, for the element of variety, in many a trapping party, not to name the summer rendezvous of the trappers, or the exploring parties of Colonel Fremont. To be sure the Chinamen and the Kanackers were a new feature in society. But whether it be in the many nationalities represented, or in the pleasures they pursued, except that in San Francisco there was a lavishness in the expenditure of wealth commensurate with its speedier accumulation, there was little new to him, and while he saw its magic growth with glad surprise, the attractions this city offered could not allure him. Nor could the vista it opened up of a chance to rise into position in the advancing struggles for political ascendency, induce one wish to locate his home in a spot so wanting in the kindly social relationships; for he had tried the things and found them vanity and vexation of spirit, and now he yearned for his mountain home, and the sweet pastoral life which it afforded in his circle of tried friends.

He saved the money he had secured by the sale of his flocks, and went down overland to Los Angeles to meet Maxwell, who took the trip by sea, which Carson having tasted once, could not be persuaded to try again, and there renewing his outfit, and visiting again some of its honored citizens, they started homeward, and had a pleasant passage till they reached the Gila River, where grass became so scarce that they were compelled to take a new course in order to find food for their horses: but Carson had no difficulty in pursuing a measurably direct course, and without encountering a snow storm, often terribly severe in the mountains of this interior country, he reached Taos on the third of December 1853.

He here received the unexpected information that he had been appointed Indian agent for New Mexico, and immediately wrote and sent to Washington the bonds of acceptance of this office. And now commences Carson's official career, in a capacity for which he was better fitted than any other person in the Territory.

Long had the Indians in his vicinity called him " father," but now he had a new claim to this title, for he was to be to them the almoner of the bounty of the United States Government. There was immediate call for the exercise of the duties of his office (for the Indians of New Mexico had all buried the tomahawk and calumet), in visiting and attempting to quiet a band of Apaches, among whom he went alone, for they all knew him, and secured from them plenty of promises to do well; but he had scarcely left them, before they were tired of the self-imposed restraint, and renewedly continued their depredations, and several serious battles were fought with them by the United States troops, the first having proved unsuccessful, but never was success wanting when the commander of United States dragoons had placed his confidence in the advice, and followed the suggestions of Kit Carson, who was admitted by them to be the prince of Indian fighters—though he never tolerated cruelty or the expenditure of life when there was no imperious necessity, but yet regarded severe measures better than a dawdling policy.

There had been serious fights in New Mexico in 1846, while Carson was away with Fremont; and it was better so, as the Mexicans were his blood and kin; yet, in the change of authority, he fully sympathized. But now, the enemy was the different tribes of Indians, and in the capacity of Agent for them, Carson chose to impress them with the power of the government for which he acted for their own good, that they might be induced to desist from their plundering, and be prepared for the influences and practises of civilization; and all the victories secured over them were due, as history truly records, "To the aid of Kit Carson," "With the advice of Kit Carson;" and never once is his name associated with a defeat; for, if he made a part of an expedition, a condition must be, that such means should be employed as he knew would accomplish the end desired; for he did not choose, by one single failure, to give the Indians a chance to think their lawlessness could escape its merited retribution.

Nor yet did Carson ever advise that confidence in the promises of the Indians which was not backed by such exhibition of power as to command obedience; knowing that with these children of the forest, schooled in the arts of plunder, and the belief that white men and white men's property were an intrusion on their hunting grounds, and therefore lawful prey—this was and is *their law*—non-resistance would not answer, and only stern command, backed by the rifle, ever has secured obedience—though they appreciate the kindnesses done by those friends who have such reliance. But it was Carson's opinion that the country cannot be safe while the Indians roam over it in this wild way, or until they are located on lands devoted to them and theirs for permanent homes, and are compelled to settle upon and cultivate the soil, when he thinks they will come, by careful teaching, to display sentiments of responsibility for their own acts.

There is little doubt that, had Carson been appointed Superintendent of Indian Affairs for the department of New Mexico, the reliance sometimes placed on treaties would have been discarded, and measures taken at an earlier date, to locate the Apaches and Comanches and Utahs, which might have been accomplished with less expenditure of blood and of treasure; but he quietly pursued his business, relying upon the influence which his knowledge and skill had given him to induce his superiors in official authority to undertake such measures as seemed to him the wisest.

The headquarters of his Indian agency were at Taos, and while he spent as much of his time as possible at Rayedo, the duties of his office compelled the larger part of it at Taos. The thousand kindly acts he was able to perform for the Indians, by whom he was constantly surrounded, had secured such regard for himself that he needed no protection where he was known—and what Indian of New Mexico did not know him? He went among them, and entertained them as the children of his charge, having their unbounded confidence and love.

Every year, in the heyday of the season, Carson continued the custom of a revival of earlier associations, by indulging, for a few days, or perhaps weeks, in the chase; and was joined in these excursions by a goodly company of his old compeers, as well as later acquired friends, and men of reputation and culture, from whatever quarter of the world, visiting the territory; and especially by a select few of the braves of the Indian tribes under his charge. These were seasons of grateful recurrence, and their pleasures were long anticipated amid the wearisome duties of his office.

The incidents of his everyday life, intervening his appointment as Indian agent and the rebellion, would furnish an abundance of material for a romance even stranger than fiction. A life so exciting as that among the Indians and brave frontiersmen, and a name so renowned as that of Christopher Carson, could not but attract and concenter wild and romantic occurrences. His life during these years is inseparably connected with the history of the Territory of New Mexico, which, could it be given to the public in all its copious and interesting details, would unquestionably concede to him all the noblest characteristics in man.

The treaties between the United States and the Indians, during the term of his appointment, were mainly the result of his acquaintance with the Indians, his knowledge of their character, and his influence over them. Nor did the Government fail to recognize his valuable services. During the rebellion, and while serving principally in New Mexico, where he distinguished himself by his untiring prosecution of hostilities with his savage foes, then at war with the Government, he was promoted from rank to rank, until he finally reached that of Brevet Brigadier-General.

In a report to the National headquarters, dated at Camp Florilla, near Fort Canby, N. M., January 26, 1864, we find the following detailed account of operations in New Mexico:

"The culminating point in this expedition has been reached at last by the very successful operations of our troops at Cañon de Chelly. Colonel Kit Carson left Fort Canby on the sixth instant with a command of four hundred men, twenty of whom were mounted. He had a section of mountain artillery with him, and taking the road *via* Puebla, Colorado, he started for Cañon de Chelly. He gave orders to Captain Pheiffer with his command of one hundred men to enter the cañon at the east opening, while he himself intended to enter it at the 'mouth,' or west opening, and by this movement he expected that both columns would meet in the cañon on the second day, as it was supposed to be forty miles in length.

"Captain Pheiffer's party proceeded two days through the cañon, fighting occasionally; but although the Indians frequently fired on them from the rocky walls above, the balls were spent long before they reached the bottom of the cañon, which, in many places, exceeded one thousand five hundred feet in depth. It was a singular spectacle to behold. A small detachment of troops moving cautiously along the bottom of one of the greatest cañons on the globe (the largest is in Asia, I believe), and firing volleys upward at hundreds of Navajoes, who looked, on the dizzy height above them, like so many pigmies. As they advanced the cañon widened in places, and various spots of cultivated land were passed, where wheat, maize, beans, melons, etc., had been planted last year; while more than a thousand feet above their heads they beheld neat-looking stone houses built on the receding ledges of rocks, which reminded the beholder of the swallows' nests in the house eaves, or on the rocky formation overhanging the 'sea-beat caves.' Further on, an orchard containing about six hundred peach-trees was passed and it was evident that the Indians had paid great attention to their culture.

"On the second day a party from Colonel Carson's column met the Captain in the cañon, and returned with him to Colonel Carson's camp. A party from the Colonel's command had, in the meantime, attacked a party of Indians, twenty-two of whom were killed. This had a dispiriting effect on many others, who sent in three of their number under a white flag. Colonel Carson received them, and assured them that the Government did not desire to exterminate them, but that, on the contrary, the President wished to save and civilize them ; and to that end General Carlton had given him instructions to send all the Navajoes who desired peace to the new reservation on the Rio Pecos, where they would be supplied with food for the present, and be furnished with implements, seeds, etc., to cultivate the soil. They departed well-satisfied, and Colonel Carson immediately ordered Captain A. B. Carey, Thirteenth United States Infantry, with a battalion to enter the cañon, and make a thorough exploration of its various branches, and at the same time to be in readiness to chastise any body of hostile Navajoes he might encounter, and to receive all who were friendly and who wished to emigrate to the new reservation. Captain Carey during a passage of twenty-four hours through a branch of the cañon hitherto unexplored, made an exact geographical map of this terrible chasm, and discovered many side cañons hitherto unknown. About one hundred Indians came in to him and declared that 'the Navajo nation was no more;' that they were tired of fighting and nearly starved, and that they wished to be permitted to advise their friends and families in the mountains; many of whom were willing to leave the land forever, and go to a country where they would be cared for and protected. They said they understood agriculture, and were certain they would make comfortable homes on the Pecos. This was, of course, only the opinion of some; others would prefer to remain and culture the soil on which they were born, and live at peace with the territory. However, the latter were positively informed that unless they were willing to remove they had better not come in, and, moreover, that the troops would destroy every blade of corn in the country next summer.

"On the 20th of January Colonel Carson came to Fort Canby, and about six hundred Indians had collected there; but when the wagons arrived to remove them only one hundred wished to go, and the remainder desired to return to their villages and caves in the mountains, on pretense of bringing in some absent member of their families. Colonel Carson very nobly and generously permitted them to choose for themselves ; but told them if ever they came in again they should be sent to Borgue Redondo, whether willing or not. Colonel Carson himself took the Indians to Santa Fé, and will remain absent about a month. Since his departure many Indians came in and agreed to go to the reservation.

" I think the Colonel foresaw this, as no person understands Indian character better than he does. Captain A. B. Carey, Thirteenth Infantry, commanding in his absence, will see that all Indians coming in will be removed, and, I think before April next, if the present good feeling exists, we shall have accomplished the removal of the entire tribe. Captain A. B. Carey, after successfully marching through the cañon and noting its topography, reached Fort Canby on the eighteenth instant, and relieved Captain Francis M'Cabe, First New Mexico Cavalry, who commanded in the absence of Colonel Kit Carson.

"As the Navajo expedition is now entirely successful, it is but justice to the officers and men of the First Cavalry of New Mexico, and to Colonel Christopher Carson and his staff to say that they have all acted with zeal and devotion for the accomplishment of that great desideratum—the removal of the Navajoes. Cut off from the enjoyments of civilized life, deprived of its luxuries, comforts, and even many of its necessaries, and restricted to the exploration of a wilderness and the castigation of an army of savages, who defied them, and endeavored to find a shelter among the cliffs, groves, and cañons of their country; in pursuing them to their haunts they have encountered appalling difficulties, namely: want of water, grass, and fuel; often exposed to the merciless fury of the elements, and to the bullets and arrows of a hidden foe. In the face of these difficulties they have discovered new rivers, springs, and mountains in a region hitherto unexplored, and penetrated by companies into the very strongholds of the enemy, who fled farther west as our columns advanced, and on various occasions the dismounted cavalry have, by rapid and unparalleled night marches, surprised that enemy, capturing his camp and securing his flocks and herds, at a time when he imagined himself far beyond our reach, and really when he occupied a country never before trodden by the foot of a white man.

"Much of the credit is due to the perseverance and courage of Colonel Kit Carson, commanding the expedition, whose example excited all to great energy, and inspired great resolution; but it may not be out of place to remark that it is now demonstrated beyond a doubt that, while the troops of New Mexico have long borne the reputation of being the best cavalry, they have proved themselves in the present campaign to be the best infantry in the world.

"General James H. Carlton, who knows, perhaps, and understands the material for an army as well as any General in our army, has directed the formation of a New-Mexican Brigade, and when the savage foe is removed, that Brigade, commanded by Brigadier-General Kit Carson, would surely reflect credit on the Territory and on the Department Commander."

After the close of the war Christopher Carson continued in the employ of the Government, rendering such services as only one equally skilled and experienced could render, until his death. He died at Fort Lyon, Colorado, on the

23a of May, 1868, from the effects of the rupture of an artery, or probably an aneurism of an artery, in the neck. But a few weeks previous he had visited Washington on a treaty mission, in company with a deputation of red men, and made a tour of several of the Northern and Eastern cities.

In his death the country has lost the most noted of that intrepid race of mountaineers, trappers, and guides that have ever been the pioneers of civilization in its advancement westward. As an Indian fighter he was matchless. His rifle, when fired at a redskin, never failed him, and the number that fell beneath his aim, who can tell ! (The identical rifle which Carson used in all his scouts, during the last thirty-five years of his life, he bequeathed, just previous to his death, to Montezuma Lodge, A. F. and A. M., Santa Fé, of which he was a member.) The country will always regard him as a perfect representative of the American frontiersman, and accord to him the most daring valor, consistent kindliness, perseverant energy and truthfulness which that whole great territory, that we must still regard as lying between the civilizations, is capable of furnishing.

THE END.

www.ingramcontent.com/pod-product-compliance
Lightning Source LLC
Chambersburg PA
CBHW011340090426
42743CB00018B/3395